QUOTES OF THE PAST AND PRESENT

A Compilation of Columns
from
the *War Cry* magazine

CREST BOOKS

The Salvation Army National Publications

Published by Crest Books
The Salvation Army National Headquarters
615 Slaters Lane, Alexandria, VA 22313

Major Ed Forster, Editor-in-Chief and National Literary Secretary
Major M. Christine Poff, Assistant to the Editor-in-Chief
Judith L. Brown, Crest Books Coordinator
Lisa Jones, Cover and Interior Design

Phone: 703/684-5523
Fax: 703/302-8617

Available from The Salvation Army Supplies and Purchasing Departments
    Des Plaines, IL – (847) 937-8896
    West Nyack, NY – (888) 488-4882
    Atlanta, GA – (800) 786-7372
    Long Beach, CA – (847) 937-8896

Printed in the United States of America

Library of Congress Control Number: 2009932567
ISBN–13: 978-0-9792266-6-3

Bible translations include the New International Version (NIV), New Century (NC), New Living (NL), Living Bible (LB) and The Message (MSG).

FOREWORD

Wisdom is a gift given to us directly from God through His Word, and God uses us in turn to share His truths with others through our own observations. This collection of inspirational quotes is taken from The Salvation Army's national magazine, the *War Cry*. "Quotes of the Past and Present" has repeatedly been cited as one of the magazine's favorite columns through readers' surveys and letters to the editor.

We gain insight and affirmation through what people around us are thinking and sharing. The fact that so many of us relate to and respond to quotes may well confirm this thought. Maxims such as "An apple a day keeps the doctor away" and "Early to bed, early to rise" began as ideas and became "quotes" as people voiced these ideas and others wrote them down.

John Maxwell has shared the concept that "Leadership is influence." The quotes contained in this book have influenced those who were present to hear them "live," and it is our hope that through this book they will continue to influence others. Many of these quotes are from famous people who had some worthwhile things to say about living a rich, full life. Others are from people of more common origins who have some uncommon wisdom to share from their own life experiences. The diversity of contributors affirms that we are more alike than we sometimes think when it comes to sharing "life lessons."

Some of these quotes "from the past" go back a long way. They are from voices that have now fallen silent, but their legacy continues to this day because someone took the time to write down what they had to say. The quotes of the present, which include the dates spoken, are from contemporary Christian thinkers – many associated with The Salvation Army and its ministry.

The book has been arranged alphabetically so that you can look up a subject that may be of interest to you. If you prefer, you can just dip in wherever you like to find hopeful, encouraging thoughts to help carry you through your day.

We are not alone – God is with us, but so, too, are a cloud of witnesses who are willing to share of themselves to benefit their communities and indeed the world, through what they say.

May this collection of quotes bless and enrich your life – and the people around you as you share some of these thoughts with them.

Major Ed Forster
Editor in Chief and
National Literary Secretary
The Salvation Army, USA

> ## "He who walks with the wise grows wise."
>
> **Proverbs 13:20a (NIV)**

*I*t's been said that life is a road to be traveled, and over time it takes us along many routes. We will encounter hazards. We will discover the scenic routes that provide us with breathtaking panoramic views we never knew existed. The travel required on this road of life brings challenges that, at times, can overwhelm us. That's why the life lessons shared by others in this book give us valuable travel tips to help avoid unnecessary trouble and to encourage us along the way.

ACTIONS

We should live as though Jesus came yesterday—rose today—and will come back tomorrow.
Martin Luther

It is amazing what you can accomplish if you do not care who gets the credit.
Harry S. Truman

True merit is like a river. The deeper it is,
the less noise it makes.
Lord Halifax

No act of kindness, no matter how small, is ever wasted.
Aesop

Always be a little kinder than necessary.
James M. Barrie

When I'm concerned about something, I figure out a plan of
action and I give it to God. I just ask to be carried through it.
God has never failed me yet.
Condoleezza Rice

If we are to better the future, we must
disturb the present.
Catherine Booth

Civil law judges overt action first, intention second;
but spiritual law always reverses the two.
Sally Chesham

It is easier to preach ten sermons than it is to live one.
Church sign

It offends God when we talk ugly.
Corps Sergeant-Major Cotton Presley
August 3, 2007

**There should be continuity between what we do on Sunday
and what we do on Tuesday.**
Reverend Jonathan Millard
September 3, 2006

The smallest mouse can bring down the house.
Reverend Howard Roy
January 9, 2009

**Regret for things we did can be tempered by time; it is
regret for the things we did not do that is inconsolable.**
Sydney J. Harris

**Some people are kind, polite, and sweet-spirited
until you try to sit in their pews.**
Church sign

ADVERSITY

In times like these, it helps to recall that there have always been times like these.
Paul Harvey

If we had no winter, the spring would not be so pleasant; if we did not sometimes taste of adversity, prosperity would not be so welcome.
Anne Bradstreet

When the winds come and chaos becomes the norm, our true colors shine in the middle of the storm.
John Zeller
September 13, 2008

God can make the malady of your heart a melody.
Bill Van Sickle

A pearl is formed by years of an oyster's irritation, but eventually it becomes a pearl of great price.
Captain Wendy Morris
February 17, 2008

Going through something with Jesus is a lot different than going through something without Jesus.
Major Joan Canning
September 3, 2008

We can be confident in God in the midst of dangers. When we truly take refuge in God, what can we fear?
Captain Chris Sanford
July 6, 2003

When you get to your wit's end, you'll find that God lives there.
Knotty Mouse

God promises a safe landing, not a calm passage.
Church Sign

Adversity introduces a man to himself.
Anonymous

Anxiety

Fear defeats more people than any other
one thing in the world.
Ralph Waldo Emerson

If the Lord be with us, we have no cause to
fear. His eye is upon us, His arm is over us,
His ear is open to our prayer.
Andrew Murray

It is not so much that we're afraid to change or
so in love with the old ways, but it's that place in between
that we fear. It's like being between trapezes. It's Linus
when his blanket is in the dryer.
There's nothing to hold on to.
Marilyn Ferguson

People aren't reluctant about change; it's the losses and
endings they are reluctant to embrace.
Dr. Dan Reiland
October 7, 2001

Fear destroys peace of mind and robs life of love, rest, and beauty.
Florence Booth

Never worry worry, until worry worries you.
Lt. Colonel Royston Bartlett
November 8, 2001

I was looking at an aerosol can this week and saw the words "Contents under pressure." Some of us should have this pasted on our foreheads.
Captain Geffory Crowell

Don't let your worries get the best of you. Remember that Moses started out as a basket case.
Anonymous

ATTITUDE

Pessimism is the cleverness of the weak. Optimism is the
courage of the strong.
Winston Churchill

Our life is what our thoughts make it.
Marcus Aurelius

The longer I live, the more convinced I have become
that life is 10% of what happens to us and 90%
how we respond to it.
Charles Swindoll

If you don't like something, change it. If you can't change it,
change your attitude.
Maya Angelou

We cannot think low thoughts and expect
to perform high actions.
Bramwell Tripp

We have two choices when facing life's crisis—we can either be bitter or we can be better.
Mary Israel

Our attitude toward life determines life's attitude toward us.
Earl Nightingale

Your living is determined not so much by what life brings to you as by the attitude you bring to life.
John Homer Miller
November 4, 2007

Some people complain because God put thorns on roses, while others praise Him for putting roses among thorns.
Nate Carter

Outlook often determines outcome.
General Bramwell Tillsley (Ret.)
July 28, 2007

People who depend on ideal circumstances are going to be miserable most of the time.
Major Joan Canning
September 3, 2008

The world looks different when we see it through "wonder eyes" and with a sense of awe.
Lt. Colonel Helen Starrett
August 30, 2006

Whines are made from gripes. Whatsoever you sow that shall you also reap.
Major David Laeger

> "It was through what His Son did that God cleared a path for everything to come to Him."
>
> Colossians 1:20a (LB)

We will undoubtedly reach junctures along life's pathways when the road gets bumpy. Sudden jolts will require some flexibility on our part as we slow our speed and even stop altogether at times. Lanes can end unexpectedly when we run into problems that test our coping skills. Although we may feel lonely and trapped with no exit, these experiences can make us stronger, more resilient and more compassionate people. Instead of yielding to frustration when we notice road-work ahead, we can focus on the joy we will feel when we reach our destination.

THE BIBLE

It is impossible to rightly govern the world without God or the Bible.
George Washington

I do not believe there is a problem in this country or the world today that could not be settled if approached through the teaching of the Sermon on the Mount.
Harry S. Truman

Nothing less than the whole Bible can make a whole Christian.
A.W. Tozer

I'm not concerned with things that I don't understand in the Bible—I'm concerned with what I do.
Mark Twain

I've read the last chapter of the Revelation, and we won!
Billy Graham

Knowledge of the Bible is worth nothing unless it is translated into action in our lives.
Samuel Logan Brengle

The morality of the Bible is, after all, the safety of society.
F.C. Monfort

The Bible is the textbook of humanity and the road map of Christian pilgrims.
Jack Madahgian

No one ever graduates from Bible study, until he meets its author face to face.
Everett Harris

Ignorance of Scripture is ignorance of Christ.
Dr. Roger Green

When I read the Bible, I receive an impression in my spirit.
Sharon Barber
August 16, 2006

If the Bible is not the unique revelation of God to fallen men and women, then there is no such revelation anywhere.
James Montgomery Boice

**Training by the book is a good idea,
as long as it is the "good" book.**
Bill Van Sickle

**It is impossible to know the wonder of God's love until you
have experienced the power of God's Word.**
*Charlie DeLeo
April 28, 2009*

I'm reading the Bible and behaving it.
A Korean student studying in America

**When you read the Bible and it moves you, that's because
that's the way the Creator made you.**
*Major Donna Hood
December 18, 2007*

**When we read Scripture we notice God doesn't build
bridges—He parts the waters or helps us go
through the currents of life.**
*Captain Geffory P. Crowell
August 8, 2007*

The Bible captures an album of snapshots of what God has done for us through the love of Jesus.
Colonel David Jeffrey
February 25, 2009

The biblical woman caught in adultery was a ping-pong ball batted back and forth between the Savior and the Jesus haters.
Major Gary Haupt
May 13, 2008

Mary and Martha were alike in one way—they both loved the Savior more than anything else.
Captain Jacqueline Hallock
October 1, 2006

Without the Scriptures we would be lost. The Scriptures give direction, correction, challenge, command, hope, explanation and foundation for living. Scripture is God's truth for His world.
International Spiritual Life Commission

BLESSING

One of the most exciting aspects of pursuing God's blessings is learning to see what He is doing around you at all times.
Bruce Wilkerson

You cannot buy a blessing. It only comes to you from God, but we must be persistent if we want to receive it.
Major Yvon Alkintor
October 5, 2008

We always have a choice between misery and blessing.
Major Cheryl Miller
October 4, 2006

BUSYNESS

Being busy does not always mean real work!
Thomas Edison

The blessings and joys of walking with Jesus are crowded out by the myriad tiny details of life.
John MacArthur

Only an uncluttered heart is fit for divine occupancy.
Commissioner Israel Gaither
August 3, 2008

Busyness is a good excuse for not dealing with the real "first things" in our lives.
Major Linda Jones
May 14, 2006

> *"You have made known to me the paths of life; you will fill me with joy in your presence."*
>
> Acts 2:28 (NIV)

Modern marvels of entertainment—DVDs, MP3 players, headphones, laptop games and videos—have replaced more basic travel games of yesteryear. Gone are the days when the monotony of the road was broken by being the first to spot an alliterative storefront: *"I see Cleo's Clip and Curl." "How about Big Bob's Bop Burger?"* The joy found in those simple games was in the sharing. Trips together mean listening to one another, joking together, and taking the time to express care and love. That same love motivated people to share some of the important ideas they gleaned from their own journeys.

CHARACTER

Whatever you are, be a good one.
Abraham Lincoln

A clean conscience makes every day like Christmas.
Poor Richard's Almanac

Try not to become a man of success, but rather to become
a man of value.
Albert Einstein

A capacity to change is indispensable.
Equally indispensable is the capacity to hold fast
to that which is good.
John Foster Dulles

Character cannot be developed in ease and quiet.
Only through experiences of trial and suffering can
the soul be strengthened, vision cleared, ambition inspired
and success achieved.
Helen Keller

Reputation is what people think of us; character is what
God and the angels know of us.
Thomas Paine

What lies behind us and what lies before us are tiny matters
compared to what lies within us.
Oliver Wendell Holmes

A stick that is about straight is crooked.
Sallie Chesham

In the long run we shape our lives and shape ourselves. The process never ends . . . And the choices we make are ultimately our own responsibility.
Eleanor Roosevelt

Only God knows the potential of a life well lived.
Joseph Stowell

What makes you worthwhile is who you are, not what you do.
Marianne Williams

You take care of your character and God will take care of your reputation.
Albert Orsborn

A true measure of a man is not in his beginnings, but in his endings.
Lt. Colonel John Falin
January 23, 2008

Long ago I learned the truth of a man is known not by how he acts when he is in control, but how he reacts when things are beyond his control.
Major Mark Welsh

**Much more is born out of our character than
out of our performance.**
Commissioner Lawrence R. Moretz
September 17, 2007

**The condition of our heart soil will always
reveal our character.**
Lt. Colonel Helen Starrett
May 13, 2009

**God is more interested in our character than our comfort
or convenience.**
Commissioner David Edwards
January 21, 1996

CHRISTIANITY

**The Church exists to set up in the world a new sign which is
radically dissimilar to the world's own manner and which
contradicts it in a way full of promise.**
Karl Barth

The closer we come to the pattern given by Jesus, the more and more important other people become to us.
George Carpenter

The chief dangers that confront the coming centuries will be religion without the Holy Spirit; Christianity without Christ; forgiveness without repentance; salvation without regeneration; politics without God; and heaven without hell.
William Booth

Christianity is freeing to me. There were many choices in life that I didn't have to make because I chose Jesus.
Major Florence Forster
March 22, 2006

Denial, carrying a cross and following Jesus does not seem like a recipe for happiness in the 21st century, but it is and will last longer than the lottery jackpot.
Captain Dean Pallant

Some people have given up on Christianity because they don't like Christians.
Major Donna Hood
March 11, 2009

The problem with the Christian life is that it is to be lived among non-Christians.
Major Mark Herbert
February 15, 2004

When the world would call us (the Church) irrelevant we must affirm that we serve God and God alone.
Major Peter Ayling
May 13, 2004

I'm glad I put myself up for adoption into God's family, and I'm glad there weren't extensive background checks made on me.
Major Peter Smith
July 24, 2009

CHRISTIANS

The Christ you see is the Christian you'll be.
Nolan Clark
November 25, 2001

There are so many Christians who do not appreciate
the magnificent dignity of their vocation to sanctify,
to the knowledge, love and service of God.
Thomas Merton

A vital fringe benefit of being a Christian is the tremendous
sense of identity that grows out of
knowing Jesus Christ.
Dr. James Dobson

Christians are a part of the song of the redeemed.
Captain Kenneth Argot
July 8, 2007

Our lives should be a reflection of Jesus Christ.
As children of God, we need to imitate Him.
Major William Bamford

We need peace and harmony in our country. As a citizen
and as a person my challenge is to seek both, but first and
foremost for me is to remain in Christ.
Captain Allister Smith
May 9, 2002

**Christians are the spiritual storehouse for a
spiritually hungry nation.**
Captain Kenneth Argot
November 23, 2008

**Every Christian is called to be a missionary.
"All the world" starts in places near to us,
where we work, study and play.**
Major Randall Sjögren

**How can Christians help fix a broken world? They can
do so by living holy lives in an unholy world.**
Commissioner Kay Rader

CHURCH

**You know who gives me the most trouble
as a pastor—just myself.**
A. W. Tozer

No church can afford to be a "non-prophet" organization.
A church bulletin board

**If the church needs a better pastor, it only needs to
pray for the one it has.**
Source unknown

COMPASSION

**Sometimes all a person needs is a hand to hold and a heart
to understand.**
Andy Rooney

**Treat a man as he appears to be and you make him worse.
But treat him as if he were what he potentially could be, and
you make him what he should be.**
Goethe

Man knows no sorrow like the lack of a loving heart.
Charlie DeLeo

When the bottom drops out [of your world] wounded people need a place to cry, a person to care, someone to bind up their wounds, someone to listen.
Charles Swindoll

It is our intention not to leave a wounded soul behind us.
Captain Christine Anderson
June 10, 2006

Put into practice a deep concern for another's suffering. Love puts it all together.
Major Doug Browning
May 24, 2006

Open our eyes, Lord, that we may see the true feelings of immigrants behind their smiles.
Major Evelyne Gosteli-Porret
May 13, 2004

We should have the tenderness of Mother Teresa and the conviction of Desmond Tutu.
Commissioner Paul du Plessis
March 27, 2003

We have all had our storms, but we also need to be aware of the storms that others are going through.

Major Sandra Defibaugh
April 11, 2007

COOPERATION

God sees our work equally whatever we do. We are partners—there is no difference between the one who plants and the one who waters.

Commissioner Makoto Yoshida
March 4, 2004

If enough spiders unite—they can tie up a lion.

An Ethiopian Proverb

Partnership means belonging to each other—it also means sharing pain and joy.

Commissioner Makoto Yoshida
March 4, 2004

COURAGE

If a man hasn't discovered something that he will die for, he isn't fit to live.
Martin Luther King, Jr.

Courage is doing what you're afraid to do. There can be no courage unless you're scared.
Eddie Rickenbacker

Courage is fear that has said its prayers.
Maya Angelou

Courage is grace under pressure.
Ernest Hemingway

If you are not facing risk, could it be that you are not close enough to where God wants you to be? Because where God is, there is always risk.
Major Ralph Bukiewicz
May 19, 2002

CREATIVITY

Anything constructed can only be appreciated after
it is constructed, but anything created is loved
from its inception.
Charles Dickens

Every man's work, whether it be literature, or music,
or pictures, or architecture, or anything else, is always
a portrait of himself.
Samuel Butler

God gave me this talent, and the least I can do is
give it back to Him.
Mahalia Jackson

Creativity is allowing yourself to make mistakes. Art is
knowing which ones to keep.
Scott Adams

God doesn't give people talents that He doesn't want people to use.
Iron Eagle

The key is what is within the artist. The artist can only paint what she or he is about.
Lee Krasner

No artist is perfect, but you need to strive for excellence.
Ferd Petrie

Anyone who buries his or her talents is making a grave mistake.
Source Unknown

CULTURE

The Western dream is to have a lot of money, and then you can lead a life of leisure and happiness. Nothing in my experience could be further from the truth.
Michael Phillips

Babel was a stupid and arrogant attempt to build a culture without God. We are living in the wreckage of those tower builders.
Ann Paton
February 17, 2008

We're getting too man–centered and not enough God–centered.
General Eva Burrows (Ret.)
July 27, 2007

> "But I'll take the hand of those who don't know the way, who can't see where they're going. I'll be a personal guide to them, directing them through unknown country."
>
> Isaiah 42:16a (MSG)

When it's time to take a trip, the most important thing to establish is where we are going. Is it a short trip to a nearby town or is it a cross-country trip? Knowing this will help determine what preparations need to be made. It's not wise to merely strike out into the unknown without a destination in mind. After all if we don't know where we're headed, we won't know when we have arrived! These observations can help us keep our destination in focus.

DEATH

The true tomb of the dead is the heart of the living.
Jean Cocteau

When our days are gone we'll find death is not
night at all, but breaking sun.
Evangeline Booth

Death has a way of interrupting our lives.
Major George Hood
April 9, 2009

A believer's death may go unnoticed, but it's
front-page news in heaven.
Source Unknown

DISCIPLESHIP

To follow Jesus means that we can't separate what Jesus is
saying from what Jesus is doing and the
way that He is doing it.
Eugene Peterson

Christianity without discipleship is always
Christianity without Christ.
Dietrich Bonhoeffer

In the spiritual life only one thing produces genuine joy and that is obedience.
Richard Foster

One can believe in the divinity of Jesus Christ and feel no personal loyalty to Him at all—indeed, pay no attention whatever to His commandments and His will for one's life.
Catherine Marshall

At its heart, discipleship is obedience.
Julia L. Roller and Lynda L. Graybeal

If Christ does not reign over the mundane events in our lives, He does not reign at all.
Paul Tripp

I dare not say with Paul that I am the slave of Christ, but my highest aspiration and desire is to be the slave of Christ.
George MacDonald

The Christian ideal has not been found tried and wanting; it has been found difficult and untried.
G.K. Chesterton

If thou art willing to suffer no adversity, how wilt thou be the friend of Christ?
Thomas à Kempis

If you have not chosen the Kingdom of God first, it will in the end make no difference what you have chosen instead.
William Law

Until you have given up yourself to Him you will not have a real self.
C. S. Lewis

It is only by a total death to self we can be lost in God.
Jeanne Guyon

The invitation is not, "Give me thine head." The invitation is "Give me thine heart."
John G. Lake

Let no one imagine that he will lose anything of human dignity by this voluntary sell-out of his all to his God. In exalting God over all, he finds his own highest honor upheld.
A. W. Tozer

A boy who rises at 4:30 to deliver papers is considered a go-getter, but to urge our young people to rise at 5:30 to pray is considered fanaticism.

Leonard Ravenhill

I surrendered unto Him all there was of me—everything! Then for the first time I realized what it meant to have real power.

Katherine Kuhlman

DISCIPLINE

The secret of discipline is motivation.

Sir Alexander Paterson

Be diligent in your approach to God.

Major Steve Morris
March 18, 2009

What is the thirst that drives you today?

Lt. Colonel Dan Starrett
April 7, 2009

What we do on some great occasions will probably depend upon what we already are, and what we are will be the result of previous years of self-discipline.

H. P. Liddon

The deadliest disease of contemporary life is impatience ... there's one thing we can't achieve over night: the discipline of righteousness.

Joshua Choonmin Kang

Christians are training to become like Christ for the rest of their time on earth.

Major Todd Hawks
November 7, 2007

When a person is sufficiently motivated, the discipline will take care of itself.

Anonymous

> "And a highway will be there; it will be called the Way of Holiness. The unclean will not journey on it; it will be for those who work in that Way; wicked fools will not go about on it."

Isaiah 35:8 (NIV)

Sometimes we reach a crossroad, confronted with a major decision that can change the course of our lives. We may decide to marry, change careers, or move to a new area after we retire. As people of faith, we pray that God will speak to us and reveal His will. Most of the time, however, we will not have a clear-cut road map to guide us every step of the way. Our personal relationship with God can serve as a GPS system, keeping us on the right path. We can still be within the will of God without knowing exactly what God wants us to do every step of the way.

EDUCATION

Education is the drawing out of the soul.
Ralph Waldo Emerson

It is the supreme art of the teacher to awaken joy in creative expression and knowledge.
Albert Einstein
May 30, 2008

Every Sunday school teacher is just as much called of God as a missionary to the heart of Africa. He needs to prepare just as diligently—he needs to labor just as earnestly—as if he were carrying the Gospel to the most remote spot on the globe.
Billy Graham

Education is learning what you didn't even know you didn't know.
Daniel Boorstin

If you think education is expensive, you ought to try ignorance.
Derek Bok

The more we learn, the more we learn that we have more to learn.
Major G. Howard Palomaki
February 20, 2007

EMOTIONS

The best and most beautiful things in the world cannot be
seen, nor even touched, but just felt in the heart.
Helen Keller

Anyone can be angry. That is easy. But to be angry
with the right person, to the right degree, at the
right time, for the right purpose and in the right way—that is
not easy.
Aristotle

Anger is only one letter short of danger.
Bill Van Sickle

It is among the wealthy that we can find the most terrible
poverty of all—loneliness.
Mother Teresa

You cannot have Jesus without giving up your pride.
Major Donna Hood

The soul hardly ever realizes it, but loneliness is really homesickness for God.
Hubert van Zellar

Grief is a powerful thing. It's a good thing. It's a way to let go of a lot of pain. But it's something to go through, not to hold on to.
From the television program Touched By An Angel

Frightened people often hide behind anger.
Source Unknown

We never know when our disappointment will be His appointment.
Charles Swindoll

Sometimes our hearts quit on our jobs, on our spouses and on our ministries, but God wants us to know that we aren't alone, and that we don't need to be discouraged.
Sharon Barber
February 13, 2008

You can tell how big a person is by what it takes to discourage him.
Source Unknown

Encouragement

We are not primarily put on this earth to see through one another, but to see one another through.
Peter DeVries

Each day comes bearing its own gifts. Untie the ribbons.
Ruth Ann Schabacker

Maybe sometimes we need to be the ones who point out the rainbows in life to others who are too busy to see them.
Lt. Colonel Joy Taylor
February 25, 2003

An ounce of encouragement is worth a pound of explanation.
Major Ed Forster

ENDURANCE

Never give up. Never, never give up.
Never, never, never give up!
Winston Churchill

Hero: An ordinary individual who finds strength to persevere
in spite of overwhelming obstacles.
Christopher Reeves

Endurance is not just the ability to bear a hard
thing but to turn it into glory.
William Barclay

One thing God accomplished in my life is the spirit of
endurance. Since God gave me this spirit I have
been a terror to Satan.
Major Caroline Ajubiga
May 9, 2002

Never Give Up! That's a final solution
to the temporary problem.
An Auschwitz Survivor

ETERNAL LIFE

Life from the center is a life of unhurried peace
and power. It is simple. It is serene. It is amazing,
It is triumphant. It is radiant. It takes no time,
but it occupies all our time.
Thomas Kelly

What a person believes about immortality will color his
thinking in every area of life.
John Sutherland Bonnell

Eternity is not something that begins after you're dead. It's
going on all the time. We are in it now.
Charlotte Perkins Gilman

What about the "hereafter"?
The after depends on the here.
Major Don Osman

EVANGELISM

We are pencils in the hand of a writing God—writing love letters to be sent around the world.
Mother Teresa

The stars are like celestial evangelists above who circle the earth every 24 hours shouting in every language that there is a God.
Carmen
Christian Performer

The great fact remains that, unless we are saving sinners, our very existence as an Army is not justified.
Catherine Bramwell Booth

The world isn't on the right path, and if we don't like it we need to help change it.
Cadet Raymond Knous
August 6, 2006

The living are dying to hear the words of Christ.
Major George Polarek
April 4, 2009

Our helping fields must become our harvest fields.
Commissioner Lawrence R. Moretz
March 18, 2004

When I go to school assemblies, I may not be able to preach the Gospel, but if you ask the right questions, some young student will do it for you.
Major Christine Clement
September 4, 2003

Help us, Lord, not just to speak the Good News, but to be the Good News.
Major Alan Lyne
May 18, 2003

Some day you may be chosen to do something weird and wild and wonderful. But it can happen every day as we spread the good news of God through gentleness, kindness and compassion.
Captain Stephen Yoder
March 7, 2002

Be fishers of men. You catch them—He'll clean them.
Church Sign

Some people stand at the pulpit but don't preach from the right place.
Source Unknown

EVIL

Children of God are being literally devoured by Satan in sexual trafficking.
Lisa Thompson
September 26, 2007

All of Satan's apples have worms.
Bill Van Sickle

Satan may tell you that you have failed so often that God will not give you the blessing. That is the devil's lie. Don't believe it.
Samuel Logan Brengle

Satan is always working to plant weeds in our spiritual garden.
Lt. Colonel Helen Starrett
May 13, 2009

The greater the evil—the greater God's grace.
Commissioner Gisèle Gowans
November 3, 2001

Goodness does not roll over and play dead when it is confronted with evil.
Lt. Colonel Eugene Pigford
September 13, 2006

Satan's only intention is to distract us from our calling.
Captain Steve Morris
February 11, 2007

The miracle is that there isn't more evil in this world than there is.
From the television program Touched By An Angel

The devil is content to let us profess Christianity as long as we do not practice it.
Source Unknown

> "But the gateway to life is very narrow and the road is difficult, and only a few ever find it."
>
> Matthew 7:14 (NL)

*T*he U.S. Army would be proud of the logistical maneuvering involved as families load the family car for vacation—sheets and towels under the seats, canned goods stacked in the wheel well, only a few change of clothes for the kids. Even a walled-off compound of blankets and luggage makes for comfortable passage for Ruff, the family cocker spaniel. It all comes down to loading only the essentials. Such careful maneuvering is required in all aspects of life for us to live wisely and well.

FAILURE

Only those who dare to fail greatly can ever achieve greatly.
Robert F. Kennedy

I have not failed. I've just found 10,000 ways that won't work.
Thomas Edison

I don't know the key to success, but the key to failure is trying to please everybody.
Bill Cosby

A man may fall many times. But he won't be a failure until he says that someone pushed him.
Elmer G. Letterman

In times such as these, it is no failure to fall short of realizing all that we might dream—the failure is to fall short of dreaming all that we might realize.
Dee Hock

We will never fail when God is involved. God doesn't expect us to be successful, but He does expect us to be faithful.
Cheryl Jones-Gage
February 27, 2006

The future need not be the pattern for the failures of the past.
General Paul Rader (Ret.)
July 28, 2007

God knows how to make yesterday's failure the
secret of today's success.
Catherine Bramwell Booth

The only way to avoid mistakes is to gain experience; the
only way to gain experience is to make mistakes.
Source Unknown

FAITH

If I were dying, and had the privilege of delivering a
last exhortation to all the Christians of the world, and that
message had to be condensed into three words,
I would say, "Wait on God!"
Samuel Logan Brengle

The greatest act of faith is when a man understands
he is not God.
Oliver Wendell Holmes

Faith is taking the first step even when you don't see the whole staircase.
Dr. Martin Luther King, Jr.

Hope is the melody of the future. Faith is the courage to dance with it.
Bishop Frey

The Gospel is too good not to believe.
Harry Dean

I will gather around my faith for light does the darkness most fear.
Jewell Kilcher and Patrick Leonard

Faith does not break loose in my head with a great hurrah for God. Believing sneaks into my soul while my head is saying, "My God, where were you when I needed you?"
Lewis Smedes

While reason gropes for answers, faith waits for God.
Joseph Bailey

Some things have to be believed to be seen.
Rudolph Hodgson

Faith is the sling that has slain many giants.
Charlie DeLeo

Faith does not minimize difficulties
but does magnify God.
General Bramwell H. Tillsley (Ret.)

You never find God until He becomes
your deepest desire.
Major Don Osman

Our faith is the preservative that helps to keep
the work going in the future.
Commissioner Reinder Schurink
September 10, 2008

Faith isn't something we get—it's something
that gets us.
Major Donna Hood
September 10, 2008

The psalmist was confident because he knew the answer—
"my help comes from the Lord!"
Commissioner Thorleif Gulliksen
March 20, 2003

Even the most devout of us sometimes put our
common sense on the altar and then put God's
name on it. What we could have instead is a deeply rooted
belief in God's deliverance.
Captain Marian Fripp
June 23, 2002

What difference would there be in your life if
you didn't have faith in God?
Captain Kenneth Argot
June 21, 2009

All the people around David were more equipped
than he was to face Goliath, but David believed
that God would deliver him and he sought God's direction
and so should we.
Major Eugene Broome
March 10, 2004

Faith sees the invisible, believes the incredible, and receives the impossible.
The Free Methodist

Here Lies An Atheist: All Dressed Up and No Place To Go
Epitaph on a gravestone

Faith is believing that something I cannot prove is truer than anything else I know and acting on that belief.
Source Unknown

FAMILY

When I was a boy of fourteen, my father was so ignorant I could hardly stand to have the old man around. But when I got to be twenty-one, I was astonished at how much the old man had learned.
Mark Twain

You don't choose your family. They are God's gift to you, as you are to them.
Desmond Tutu

Fathers are what give daughters away to other men who aren't nearly good enough, so they can have grandchildren who are smarter than anybody's.
Paul Harvey

Parents' words may fade, but the memory of their lives lasts a lifetime.
Hal Donaldson

Youth fades; love droops; the leaves of friendship fall: A mother's secret love outlives them all.
Oliver Wendell Holmes

As a mother, my job is to take care of the possible and trust God with the impossible.
Ruth Graham Bell

The mother's heart is the child's schoolroom.
Henry Ward Beecher

Perhaps the greatest earthly blessing known to man is a godly mother. No other gift has so direct a bearing on his present and everlasting well-being.

William Booth

Being a new dad is sort of like putting together IKEA furniture. You have to work it out piece by piece. The only difference is that there is no real instruction manual! That's why prayer and patience come in handy.

Geoff Moulton
November 6, 2006

A father knows what his child needs.

Sharon Barber
June 7, 2006

He can climb the highest mountain or swim the biggest ocean. He can fly the fastest plane and fight the strongest tiger. My father can do anything. But most of the time he just carries out the garbage.

an 8 year-old's view of his father

By investing in children and in the families that sustain them, the nation is ultimately investing in its own development.
Carol Bellamy
December 2000

Make a memory with your children. Spend time to show you care: Toys and trinkets can't replace those precious moments that you share.
Elaine Hardt

A father is a man who expects his son to be as good a man as he meant to be.
Frank A. Clark

When I was a kid, my father told me everyday, "You're the most wonderful boy in the world, and you can do anything you want to."
Jan Hutchins
May 17, 1988

A child must not only have something to do, something to make; there must be someone to admire the finished work.
Florence Booth

Newlyweds become oldlyweds, and oldlyweds are the reasons that families work.
Source Unknown

FORGIVENESS

He who cannot forgive others breaks the bridge over which he must pass himself, for every man needs to be forgiven.
Thomas Fuller

This is the essence of forgiveness, seeing people through the eyes and heart of a loving God.
George McDonald

No sin is too great for Christ's forgiveness.
Reverend Howard Roy
April 29, 2007

Forgiveness is not a sign of weakness, it's a sign of strength.
From the television program Touched By An Angel

Reconciliation for me means freedom—not only for the offender, but for everyone.
Captain Elsa Oalang
October 31, 2002

If we are faithful and ask God for it, He will give us a clean heart.
Major David Dickson
October 12, 2008

1 Tree + 3 Nails = 4 Given
Source Unknown

FREEDOM

Those who deny freedom for others deserve it not for themselves.
Abraham Lincoln

If a nation values anything more than freedom,
it will lose its freedom.
Somerset Maugham

The theme song of a free heart is,
"It is well with my soul."
Major Christine Poff
July 5, 2009

There are times when God sends thunder to stir us. There
are times when God sends blessings to lure us. But there
are times when God sends nothing but
silence as He honors us with the freedom to
choose where we spend eternity.
Max Lucado

The cause of freedom is the cause of God.
William Lisle Bowles

Empty religion robs us of God and the freedom to enjoy
God's presence in our lives.
Major Christine Poff
July 5, 2009

FRIENDSHIP

A friend is someone who thinks you are a good egg even if you're slightly cracked.
Bernard Meltzer

A good friend remembers what we were and sees what we can be.
Janette Oke

A friend will strengthen you with his prayers, bless you with his love, and encourage you with his hope.
Source Unknown

A true friend is one who overlooks your failures and tolerates your success.
Doug Larson

Friendships multiply joy and divide griefs.
H. G. Bohn

Friendship is the living out of the command to love.
Major Mark Tillsley
August 19, 2008

The depth of friendship can be determined by the length of time two friends can sit together comfortably in silence.
Source Unknown

FUTURE

The best thing about the future is that it comes only one day at a time.
Abraham Lincoln

We should all be concerned with the future because we are going to have to spend the rest of our lives there.
Charles Kettering

God wisely keeps from us the sight of our shattered dreams that tomorrow sometimes brings.
Clarence W. Hall

Things happen in God's time, not yours.
From the television program Touched By An Angel

> *"People with integrity walk safely, but those who follow crooked paths will slip and fall."*
>
> **Proverbs 10:9 (NL)**

We all have horror stories of road trips that went haywire because of problems with the car. Nothing cranks up the tension more between travel companions than avoidable breakdowns. Make sure the car is ready for the road. Have the oil checked. Make sure the tires are in good condition and inflated properly. Top off the window washer fluid. These seemingly insignificant steps can make the difference between cruisin' the highway with the wind at our backs and sitting by the side of the road waiting for the tow truck. Such rigorous inspection of our own viewpoints and attitudes can help us avoid emotional meltdowns as well.

GENEROSITY

Make all you can, save all you can, give all you can.
John Wesley

We cannot maintain a good life of extravagance and a good conscience simultaneously. One or the other has to be sacrificed. Either we keep our conscience and reduce our affluence by giving generously and helping those in need, or we keep our affluence and smother our conscience. We have to choose between God and man.
John Stott

The dedicated life is the life worth living. You must give with your whole heart.
Annie Dillard

The philanthropic experience is the healthiest way to live.
Douglas M. Lawson

When the woman poured the perfume on Jesus' feet, was it an act of extravagance, or an act of selflessness? What are we hoarding that we might be able to share with someone else?
Lt. Colonel Helen Starrett
March 1, 2006

Generosity consists not in the sum given, but the manner in which it is bestowed.
Source Unknown

God is a giver by nature, but His generosity is often thwarted. Who can restrain the Almighty when He wants to give? I can and you can. God's giving often is thwarted for want of a taker.
General John Gowans (Ret.)
August 29, 2002

GOD

God goes where He is wanted. He does not force Himself on an individual or on a nation, whether it be first century Jews or modern Americans.
Philip Yancey

For years we've been telling God to get out of our schools, to get out of our government and to get out of our lives. And being the gentleman that He is, I believe that He has calmly backed out. How can we expect God to give us His blessing and protection if we demand that He leave us alone?
Anne Graham

God always looks at our heart. When we have a relationship with Him, it is through a clean heart.
Jerry Duke
August 23, 2006

Regardless of the blessings you've received, God is not a celestial busboy, who without benefit of a relationship, exists solely to clean up our spills and our messes.
Harold James Marshall

The great thing about being one with God is that it doesn't depend on you.
Katie Burgmayer
March 14, 2007

Everything can change in the blink of an eye. But don't worry; God never blinks.
Regina Brett

God knows what we are, and yet still believes in what we can become.
Frederick Coutts

God is who He is, and what He says is important. I discovered I had to go as far as God was willing to take me.
Major Algerome Newsome
January 6, 2008

You'll never find God if you treat Him like a divine assistant.
Major Donna Hood
March 20, 2008

God is the goal, and our guide.
General Paul Rader (Ret.)

When Elvis Presley says "You are always on my mind" that's one thing, but when God says it—that's really something else!
General Eva Burrows (Ret.)
July 27, 2007

Isaiah's God was one who could produce new life and make the stony, waste places productive. His God was wonderful—so wonderful that He could produce streams in the desert.
Colonel Michael Pressland
October 7, 2001

Without God we are inadequate.
Captain Kenneth Argot
June 21, 2009

People have a difficult time understanding a "three-in-one" God. It isn't surprising, since most people still haven't grasped the concept of a "two-in-one" marriage.
Captain David Repass
September 27, 2007

If you have a God you can't argue with or who can't contradict you—then you have a God of your own making.
Major Donna Hood
September 13, 2006

Do we accuse God of not caring because we've already decided what His care looks like?
Major Linda Jones
May 14, 2006

It's God who cuts the road straight—we would not move an inch without His help.
Lt. Colonel Charles White
April 26, 2006

In knowing God, I'm at home.
Commissioner Sue Swanson
July 5, 2006

God has always underscored and emphasized individual involvement. He calls me personally to follow Jesus.
Lt. Colonel Joseph DeMichael
July 12, 2006

Sometimes God stops us from our movements for our own good.
Captain Kenneth Argot
June 27, 2009

God doesn't mind being disturbed. Disturb Him often.
Major Susan McMillan
January 17, 2002

GOD'S FAITHFULNESS

God can do anything except fail us.
Mark Wyman

God would rather let the stars drop out of the firmament than fail you.
Emma Booth Tucker

God will never be taken by surprise. He will prepare you now for your tomorrows.
Major Don Osman

My life is about the faithfulness of God. I am clay. What can clay do, except yield to the hands of the potter?
Major Joan Canning
July 30, 2008

Where God guides, God provides.
Source Unknown

GOD'S GOODNESS

The greatest thing about God is everything.
Charlie DeLeo

The greatness and goodness of God is humanity's constant surprise!
Jack Madahgian

There are more references in the Bible to God's holiness than to of His other attributes.
General Eva Burrows (Ret.)
July 28, 2007

God is a righteous God and He will never get to the point of accepting your sin.
Major Victor Leslie
May 20, 2007

The goodness of God is that He creates us in His image so that we can remember that we are His.
Captain Trista Collins
October 29, 2006

GOD'S LOVE

God proved His love on the Cross. When Christ hung, and bled, and died, it was God saying to the world,
"I love you."
Billy Graham

Just as there comes a warm sunbeam into every cottage window, so comes a "lovebeam" of God's care and pity for every separate need.
Nathaniel Hawthorne

Our problems are large, but our hearts are larger. Our challenges are great, but our will is greater. Our flaws are endless, but God's love is boundless.
Jimmy Carter

Couldn't let go of my faith. But what's more interesting is that I don't think God will let go of me.
Bono

Even in places where beauty is rarest, pure hearts can trace the finger of God.
Erik Leidzen

A flower that blooms today, fades tomorrow. But the beauty of God's love lasts forever.

Charlie DeLeo
July 16, 2006

When we give away God's love, more of it comes back to us.

Richard Simington

The Lord doesn't love us on the basis of who we are, but only as who we are in Him.

Sue Dodge
April 2, 2008

What we are is children of God and God has lavished us with His love.

Major Suzanne Barrington
June 24, 2007

God's love for us keeps us hopeful and our love for Him keeps us faithful.

Major Tony Barrington
May 6, 2007

God's unfailing love will not go away.
Lt. Colonel Suzanne Haupt
June 3, 2009

There is a most awful picture of hurt and pain in the world, but nothing can separate us from the love of God. Whatever the powers and dominations are, we know that Christ has overcome the world and that God is the ultimate power.
Lt. Colonel Dawn Sewell
March 16, 2004

The love of God is often expressed to us through human touch.
Major Margaret Ousey
May 25, 2003

The love of God is an offer that must be received. It is often spurned and rejected. Even among Christians it is often taken for granted.
Major Doug Jones
December 23, 2001

God is love and we are filled with the bountiful outpouring of that great measure day after day.
Commissioner Lawrence R. Moretz
February 13, 2009

The Lord is my shepherd. He leads me to green pastures—otherwise I'd stay out where there's nothing but brown, scraggy grass.
Major Tony Barrington
September 4, 2006

GOD'S PRESENCE

We are closer to God in a garden than anywhere else on earth.
Emily Dickinson

God speaks through burning bushes, braying donkeys, through rainbows and in a still small voice. It's all part of His "everywhereness."
Scott Bedio

God is not to be thought of as "out there" or "up there" but as "always here."
Harry Dean

God is not a God who is far off and detached from us.
Major Steve Morris

God is always here. Sometimes we don't see Him because we put so much clutter between God and ourselves.
Major Janys Smyth
April 13, 2004

The Lord's presence wasn't in the wind or in the fire, but in the gentle breeze.
Major Richard Gaudion
August 19, 2008

When we come into the presence of God—the darkness is gone.
Commissioner Max Feener
November 5, 2006

No vacuum is as complete as the absence of God.
Major Gary Haupt
April 1, 2009

It's a gift that God has given us that we are able to experience Him personally.
Commissioner Brian Taylor
January 29, 2004

When I am in the shadow of the Almighty—I am in the presence of God.
Major Margaret Meldrum
September 25, 2003

When things happen, God's there.
Major Ed Forster
July 1, 2009

GOD'S SOVEREIGNTY

The idea of the intrinsic rationality of the world was built into Christianity from the beginning, for everything was created by God and imbued with His harmony and order.
Jonathan Hill

The Lord ordains everything except how we are going to respond.
Major James Allison
February 15, 2009

God is alive and in control of the world's events.
Major Joan Canning
January 21, 2009

If God could look after the universe in the twinkling of an eye—He's got plenty of time for you.
General Eva Burrows (Ret.)
July 27, 2007

God—quit applying for his position and accept His power.
Major Don Osman

It is only by God's grace and power that we can do the will of God. It is He that provides the wherewithal to accomplish it.
Lt. Colonel Edith Pigford
September 12, 2006

Left to ourselves we make God so much less than He is. We restrict His power when we try to make Him what we want. We mustn't make God what we want Him to Be. He is not a made–to–order God. We mustn't make him into a shape of our own design.
Colonel Joy Cooper
November 21, 2002

The sovereign God came to us as a servant God. He was not remote. He is the God who works through all and in all, the God within us.

Major Janey Thornton
January 20, 2002

It is not always what we see that matters. Sometimes it's what we don't see. Sometimes we need to look higher to see God's majesty.

Lt. Colonel Dan Starrett
January 19, 2004

Our desire may not always intersect with our reality, but our reality always intersects with God's will.

Major Keith J. Welch

A coincidence is a small miracle in which God chooses to remain anonymous.

Source Unknown

GOSPEL

The Gospel does not consist of what we can do for
ourselves, but of what God stands ready to do for us.
Arkansas Methodist

The Christian Gospel is not about what we cannot do—but
about what we can do through the power of Christ.
General Paul Rader (Ret.)
July 28, 2007

As we preach Christ we share a gospel of truth.
Major Paul Cain
May 13, 2004

Church should be a safe place to hear
a dangerous message.
Willow Creek Church slogan

We don't change the message; the message changes us.
Christian Bumper Sticker

GOSSIP

Gossip needn't be false to be evil—there's a lot of truth that shouldn't be passed around.
Frank Clark

Gossiping: Hearing something you like about someone you don't.
Earl Wilson

Who gossips with you will gossip of you.
Irish saying

The best thing to remember about gossip is to forget it.
Source Unknown

GRACE

All human nature vigorously resists grace because grace changes us and the change is painful.
Flannery O'Connor

With God, it isn't who you were that matters; it's who you are becoming.
Liz Curtis Higgs

The greatest challenge we face is to lead religious people to an understanding of God's grace.
Lloyd Ogilvy

He who demands mercy and shows none burns the bridges over which he himself must later pass.
Thomas Adams

Grace that is calculated and expected is no longer grace.
Captain Annalise Francis
May 6, 2007

God's grace is beyond imagination.
Source Unknown

If you're going to go deep with God—you're going to find the dangers of the desert and the dangers of the cross, but if you're willing, you're going to find greater grace than you have ever found before.
Major Tony Barrington
February 4, 2007

God's extravagant grace has always been available to me throughout my life, so, like Paul the apostle, I have always been able to be content in all circumstances.
Lt. Colonel Sharon E. Berry
May 20, 2006

The message of the payment for our sins and the joy of reconciliation can flood us again with both humility and thanksgiving.
Commissioner Lawrence R. Moretz
February 27, 2009

Jesus wants everything we do to be affected by His grace.
Major Donna Hood
March 11, 2009

The will of God never takes you where the grace of God will not protect you.
Source Unknown

GRATITUDE

As we express our gratitude, we must never forget that the highest appreciation is not to utter words, but to live by them.
John Fitzgerald Kennedy

If you want to turn your life around, try thankfulness. It will change your life mightily.
Gerald Good

How wonderful it would be if we could help our children and grandchildren to learn thanksgiving at an early age.
Sir John Templeton

God gave you a gift of 86,400 seconds today. Have you used one to say "thank you"?
William Arthur Ward

Gratitude is the memory of the heart.
Jean Baptiste Massieu

**Seeds of discouragement will not grow
in the thankful heart.**
Source Unknown

Our mission in life is to be grateful for all God has given us.
Major Sandra Defibaugh
November 14, 2007

**There's always a lot to be thankful for if you
take time to look for it.**
Major Ed Ringle
April 2, 2007

**There is one thing God can't give us—that's a grateful heart.
That's got to come from us. Our gratefulness is a gift to
God for all He has done for us.**
Major Sandra Defibaugh
November 14, 2007

**A simple word of thanks to a person who is just doing their
job can make a difference.**
Source Unknown

> *"Set up signposts to mark your trip home. Get a good map. Study the road conditions. The road out is the road back."*
>
> Jeremiah 31:21 (MSG)

We know where we're headed, but how are we going to get there? Will we be taking an interstate highway or back roads? Will we be passing through major cities or rural towns? If we are going to make an overnight stop, where is the best place along the way to do so? Are there are any attractions we want to take in along the way? These are questions to ask in order to map out the trip so that no one is disappointed or upset because we missed a stop or we are unable to find a decent place to stay for the night. Those who have traversed the same routes of the soul have left some guideposts to refresh us.

HAPPINESS

Many people have the wrong idea about what constitutes true happiness. It is not attained through self-gratification but through fidelity to a worthy cause.
Helen Keller

If one only wished to be happy, this could be easily accomplished; but we wish to be happier than other people, and this is always difficult, for we believe others to be happier than they are.
Montesquieu

Happiness is a butterfly, which, when pursued, is always just beyond your grasp, but which, if you will sit down quietly, may alight upon you.
Nathaniel Hawthorne

HOLIDAYS

I will honor Christmas in my heart, and try to keep it all the year.
Charles Dickens

The spirit of Christmas is peace, the miracle of Christmas is hope and the heart of Christmas is love.
William James

Easter says you can put truth in a grave, but it won't stay there.
Clarence W. Hall

Not what we say about our blessings, but how we use them, is the true measure of our thanksgiving.
W. T. Purkiser

True thanksgiving means that we need to thank God for what He has done for us, and not to tell Him what we have done for Him.
George R. Henrick

This nation will remain the land of the free only so long as it is the home of the brave.
Elmer Davis

The wonder of Christmas is that God who dwelt among us now can dwell within us.
Roy Lessin

We need Christmas to remind us that hope is not the prisoner of despair, but the captive of faith.
William Booth

Blessed is the season that engages the whole world in a conspiracy of love.
Hamilton Wright Mabie

In a single gift, God gave everything He had so that we would have everything we need.
Source Unknown

HOLINESS

In our era, the road to holiness necessarily passes through the world of action.
Dag Hammarskjold

Holiness is the everyday business of every Christian.
Charles Colson

Holiness consists in having something taken from us and in having our spiritual nature made over in the image of Jesus.
Samuel Logan Brengle

We're not likely to pay the price of sanctification if we think
we can get into heaven without it.
Allister Smith

Holiness is not a state you achieve; it is a hunger,
a desire you receive.
Calvin Miller
August 4, 2006

The alternative to holiness is halfy–ness.
Lyell Rader

Holiness does not come through the mind,
but through the heart.
Bill Van Sickle

Do not think you can make holiness popular. It cannot be
done. There is no such thing as holiness separate from
"Christ in you," and it is an impossibility to make Jesus
Christ popular in this world.
Samuel Logan Brengle

Spiritual values are not instantaneous. There are no shortcuts to holiness of life—no chair lift up the mountain of character.

Flora Larsson

The New Testament doctrine of holiness is one of progress, not progress to Christ so much as progress in Christ—and this rule governs the whole of the way from earth to heaven.

Frederick Coutts

Holiness is really goodness wrapped in the human frame.

Commissioner Trevor Tuck

Holiness drenches us in love which then tempers and directs our behaviors.

Major Doug Browning
October 25, 2008

Jesus tells us that the temple, that is each of us, must be cleansed.

Major Sandra Defibaugh
March 17, 2008

Holiness is like garlic—if someone has it, they don't have to tell you about it.
Commissioner Trevor Tuck
September 12, 2007

Holiness is about living our lives and allowing the expression of Christianity to show by sharing the love of God.
Captain Robert Webb
July 23, 2006

Christlikeness is the best one–word definition in the English language for holiness.
Commissioner Andrew S. Miller

Christians need more spiritual nourishment and they need to be more holy before God.
Major David Varghese
February 19, 2004

Nothing compares with the "real thing."
The "real thing" is holiness.
Lt. Colonel Joy Taylor
September 3, 2002

When I was a boy of eight I told God, I don't want to be great. I just want to be good.
Brigadier Clifford Honeyball
May 11, 2002

If you are very firmly attached at the center, you can dare to be free around the periphery.
Quaker Proverb

HOLY SPIRIT

Every gift of the Spirit that a believer may claim to possess must be judged by its power to produce a more Christ-like character.
Frederick Coutts

The companionship of the Spirit ensures a never–ending flow of refreshing power, peace and purpose.
Commissioner Israel Gaither

The Holy Spirit is a stream of water that is flowing by us at every moment, and all we need to do is soak up that water.
Captain Kenneth Argot
January 4, 2009

The work of the Holy Spirit is to take our pandemonium and give us peace.
Major David Atkinson
June 17, 2009

How empty we are when we are not Spirit–filled.
Lt. Colonel Herb Rader
May 15, 2004

When the Holy Spirit comes the will of God becomes a magnificent obsession.
Commissioner Lawrence R. Moretz
August 10, 2003

The power of The Salvation Army is not in its number of people or in its buildings, but it is in the power of the Holy Spirit working through people.
Commissioner Reinder Schurink
September 18, 2003

Atomic power was always available but it was not always recognized. It is the same with the Holy Spirit. His power is always available to believers, but it is not always recognized.

Major Graham Wood
June 8, 2003

In this world of traffic we cannot move—it is only the Spirit of God who can move us along.

Lt. Colonel Beatrice Nweke
February 20, 2003

Sometimes we can get in the way of the Holy Spirit even though we are Spirit–filled Christians.

Major Diane Payne
June 2, 2002

The keeping safe of our service is only possible through the deep, inner–refreshing presence of the Holy Spirit.

Commissioner Israel L. Gaither
July 1, 2009

HOPE

Hope keeps us from wrapping ourselves in the encumbering robes of self–pity and despair.
Sharon Robertson

The Bible is a treasure chest of hope and an arsenal of power.
Charlie DeLeo

The 400 years of silence between the Old and the New Testaments was broken by the cry of a baby. This breaking of silence brought a wonderful renewal of hope.
Major Linda Jones
December 22, 2002

The rich and the poor have this in common—they both need hope.
Major Richard Justvig
October 1, 2006

When the world says, "Give up," hope whispers, "Try one more time."
Source Unknown

Remembering engenders hope.
Major Christine Poff
November 12, 2008

The living God is my living. It is a wonderful moment when one discovers that God gives us a living hope.
Colonel Edith Löfgren
May 22, 2003

Man's way leads to a hopeless end. God's way leads to an endless hope.
Source Unknown

HUMANITY

What do we live for, if not to make the world a better place for each other?
George Elliot

Every man's life is a plan of God.
Horace Bushnell

I am the result of the handiwork of God.
Major Mark Israel
April 7, 2008

A society grows great when old men plant trees whose shade they will not see.
A Greek saying

People are funny; they want the front of the bus, the middle of the road, and the back of the church.
Church sign

HUMILITY

I have been driven many times to my knees by the overwhelming conviction that I had nowhere else to go.
Abraham Lincoln

The man who is poor in spirit is the man who knows that things mean nothing and that God means everything.
William Barclay

Remember that a pencil has to bow its head before it can correct its mistakes.
Major Fred Thornhill
March 29, 2006

When we forget about ourselves, we do things others will remember.
Our Daily Bread

HUMOR

Laughter is an instant vacation.
Milton Berle

Kids really brighten a household. They never turn off the lights.
Ralph Bus

Any a man's idea of charity is to give unto others advice
he can't use himself.
Hugh Murr

Summer is when kids slam the doors they
left open all winter.
Source Unknown

A perfect summer day is when the sun is shining,
the breeze is blowing, the birds are singing, and
the lawn mower is broken.
James Dent

I don't know why some people change churches—what
difference does it make which one you stay home from?
Church sign

A six-year-old's prayer: Dear Lord, if you're trying to make
me a better boy, don't worry about it. I kind like being
just the way I am.
Source Unknown

A laugh is worth a hundred groans in any market.
Charles Lamb

I believe in getting into hot water. I think it keeps you clean.
G. K. Chesterton

A laugh is a smile that bursts.
Mary H. Waldrip

Lord, please keep your arm around my shoulder and your hand over my mouth.
Sign on an office desk

Our God owns the kettles in a thousand malls.
Major Doug Burr
Christmas 2001

It is good if you learn to laugh at yourself because you'll never run out of material.
Source Unknown

"You have made known to me the path of life; you will fill me with joy in your presence, with eternal pleasures at your right hand."

Joshua 1:7B (MSG)

Taking a leisurely scenic route gives us time to revel in God's abundant creation. When we detour away from the traffic, noise and pollution, we remember our responsibility to care for this world. Urbanites especially need to be reminded of how our food is grown and transported to us. The beauty of lakes, oceans, rivers and mountains inspires awe and gratitude for everything that sustains us. It encourages us to protect our natural resources, and to ensure that the earth remains habitable for our children and grandchildren.

INFLUENCE

Surround yourself with people who are most like you want to be.
Steve Gilliard
April 8, 2008

Never, if possible, lie down at night without being able to say: I have made one human being, at least, a little wiser, a little happier, or a little better this day.
Charles Kingsley

A mighty man inspires and trains other men to be mighty.
Samuel Logan Brengle

Some people strengthen the society just by being the kind of people they are.
John W. Gardner

All the world is cold when we have no fire within us.
Alfred J. Gilliard

Those who bring sunshine into the lives of others cannot keep it from themselves.
James M. Barrie

A life is not important except in the impact it has on other lives.
Jackie Robinson

Get involved at some level—individuals can make a difference.
Source Unknown

Salt doesn't make an explosion into food—it makes an infusion to influence its flavor.
Captain Bethany Hawks
May 31, 2006

Everyone produces a quotation worth repeating. Even silence speaks.
Major G. Howard Palomaki
August 16, 2008

Like a pencil, Christians make an impression. Hopefully it is a mark that makes a difference for the kingdom.
Major Fred Thornhill
March 29, 2006

A good person increases the value of every other person whom he influences.
Source Unknown

Inspiration

If you have built castles in the air, your work need not be lost; that is where they should be. Now put foundations under them.
Henry David Thoreau

Enthusiasm is excitement with inspiration, motivation, and a pinch of creativity.
Bo Bennett

When we seek to discover the best in others, we somehow bring out the best in ourselves.
William A. Ward

Discontent is the first step in progress. No one knows what is in him till he tries, and many would never try if they were not forced to.
Basil W. Maturin

One must not lose desires. They are mighty stimulants to creativeness, to love and to long life.
Alexander A. Bogomoletz

Don't let other people tell you what you want.
Pat Riley

> "Your word is a lamp to my feet and a light for my path."
>
> Psalm 119:105 (NIV)

While animals rely on instinct to migrate, hibernate, forage for food and raise their young, human beings learn survival techniques from each other. God has given us the capacity to apply our abilities to learn new and better ways to live. The wisdom that comes with experience is considered in the most ancient books of the Bible as one of the most precious of attainments, more precious than silver and gold, status and fame, power and pleasure. Its light dispels the darkness of ignorance.

JESUS

Jesus really is with us, shouldering the burden with us, bearing the yoke with us. And He will show [you] how to live [your] life as He would live [your] life if He were [you].
Richard Foster

Jesus will never be all you need until Jesus is all you have.
Dr. David J. Gyertson
November 15, 1999

Life is worth the living, just because He lives.
William and Gloria Gaither

Jesus knows me, this I love.
William B. Bradbury and Fred Brock

Jesus came to establish a kingdom in the hearts of men.
Larry Grey
December 20, 2006

Christ is the referee of our troubled hearts.
Jarl Wahlstrom

Christ should be our "bread of life," but not just the crust.
Bill Van Sickle

If you're not at home with Jesus now—you can't be at home with Jesus then.
Major Mark Bell
November 19, 2008

Jesus makes the invisible visible. He makes the unknowable available to us.
Lt. Colonel Clive Adams
August 19, 2008

The "joy" came wrapped in a swaddling blanket.
Lt. Colonel John Falin
December 5, 2007

Christ comes to us in many different ways throughout our day, and we miss Him.
Lt. Colonel Dan Starrett
August 29, 2007

The line to Jesus has never been busy—it is always open. It has never had any dropped calls; it is the eternal line for the whosoever.
Major Yvon Alkintor
April 8, 2007

Jesus doesn't ever want to be an afterthought.
Captain Mike Himes
December 13, 2006

Jesus pulled us out of our defeated position and won the victory for us.
Major Joanne Senft

The debt that I couldn't pay, Jesus didn't owe.
Colonel Myrtle Ryder
June 14, 2006

The water that Jesus gives flows constantly and freely on a daily basis.
Major Dorothy Hitzka
July 19, 2006

It is in our need and weaknesses that Christ draws nearest.
Lt. Colonel Gustave Allemand
April 22, 2004

We sometimes want Jesus as a divine means for our own selfish ends.
Lt. Colonel Mike Williams
April 13, 2003

When we acknowledge Jesus as Lord of our lives, we find He has something to say about all of it—our jobs, our homes, our families. He has to be Lord of all of our lives—not just the religious bits.
Major Beverly McCombe
November 17, 2002

Jesus didn't come into this world to make me better. He came to make me new.
Major Carolee Israel
April 7, 2008

JOURNEY

Every day you may make progress. You know you will never get to the end of the journey. But this, so far from discouraging, only adds to the joy and glory of the climb.
Winston Churchill

An essential part of the journey to holiness is bringing our frenetic activity on God's behalf to a halt, and opening up time for Him to act directly.
Christopher Webb

I may not have gone where I intended to go, but I think I have ended up where I needed to be.
Douglas Adams

The man who walks with God always gets to his destination.
Rick Matthes

There is no hitchhiking in the spiritual life.
Flora Larsson

Christ's teachings are a moral compass that will lead us toward that which is right, and away from that which is wrong.
Major Alberto Suarez
February 8, 2009

Let the milestones of yesterday become a stepping stone today as you press onward and upward toward Eternity tomorrow.
Major Harry Litherland
March 2, 2009

I waited my whole life for someone to write on a wall what God's will for my life was, but that never happened. God spoke to me through other people when He called me.
Major Mike Olsen
September 18, 2003

You can't begin a new life until you're finished with the old one.
From the television program Touched By An Angel

JOY

The fullness of joy is to behold God in everything.
Julian of Norwich

There is more joy in Jesus in 24 hours than there is in the world in 365 days. I have tried them both.
R. A. Torrey

Your joy is your choice. Today I choose joy.
Major Mike Himes
December 10, 2008

Rejoice in the Lord always, and again I say rejoice—Paul was smart to say it twice because we might not have gotten it the first time.
Tabitha Gray
August 6, 2006

Each of us can be a reflection of what joy is.
Captain Bethany Hawks
February 15, 2006

> ## "I run in the path of your commands, for you have set my heart free."
>
> **Psalm 119:32 (NIV)**

Packing well is one key to a successful trip. The type of trip we are about to take determines what needs to be packed. A ski trip requires warm clothes and ski gear. A trip to the beach means we need the swim gear. A business trip means we need to take our work with us. A vacation means we pack for fun. It's no fun to get to the destination and find that the handouts for the presentation we are going to make got left behind, or we get to the beach only to discover that the swim suits are still at home. These thoughts might help you remember what to take along so you are equipped for any journey.

KINDNESS

A kind word is like a spring day.
Russian proverb

Always be a little kinder than necessary.
James M. Barrie

How beautiful a day can be when kindness touches it!
George Elliston

No act of kindness, no matter how small, is ever wasted.
Aesop

KINGDOM OF GOD

**Don't judge each day by the harvest you reap,
but by the seeds you plant.**
Robert Louis Stevenson

**I am surrounded by priests who repeat incessantly that their
kingdom is not of this world, and yet they lay their hands
on everything they can get.**
Napoleon Bonaparte

**All Christians have eternal life, but not all
enjoy abundant life.**
Graham Scroggie

Eternal life does not begin with death; it begins with faith.
Samuel Shoemaker

I picture heaven as a great family reunion.
Scott Bedio
October 18, 2006

Heaven must be in me before I can be in heaven.
Charles Stanford

I've been reflecting on the power of the Kingdom of God recently—just let it grow and God will sort it all out in the harvest.
Lt. Colonel Victor Poke

The Kingdom of Heaven is the reign of God and the rule of God in our lives, which actually means the personal presence of Jesus.
Major Tony Barrington
July 10, 2006

> "Be strong and very courageous. Be careful to obey all the law my servant Moses gave you; do not turn from it to the right or to the left, that you may be successful wherever you go."

Joshua 1:7 NIV

*W*e need a mature faith and good boundaries in order to clarify what gives life meaning and purpose. Many of us spend our time trying to acquire the dead-end goals of money, power, and fame. Others seek meaning in achievement, which earns respect in the eyes of the world but ultimately leaves a real void. Still others lose themselves in attachments to other people, abandoning their relationship with God along the shoulder of the road. Don't be afraid to risk choosing "the road less traveled," and watch out for one-way streets that lead to nowhere on our spiritual journey.

LEADERSHIP

Leadership is about passion.
Kerri Anderson

The question, "who ought to be boss?" is like asking who ought to be the tenor in the quartet. Obviously, the man who can sing tenor.
Henry Ford

You do not lead by hitting people over the head—that's assault, not leadership.
Dwight Eisenhower

Avoid having your ego so close to your position that when your position falls, your ego goes with it.
Colin Powell

Never tell people how to do things. Tell them what to do and they will surprise you with their ingenuity.
George S. Patton

I will pay more for the ability to deal with people than any other ability under the sun.
John D. Rockefeller

The great success of William Booth was to be found in the concentration of all the forces of a very strong personality upon the achievements of a great end.
W. T. Stead

Pick battles big enough to matter, small enough to win.
Jonathan Kozol

**Rank does not confer privilege or give power.
It imposes responsibility.**
Peter Drucker

**A leader is one who sees more than others see, who sees
farther then others see, and who sees before others do.**
Leroy Eims

**It always comes back to leadership. Leadership is always
the problem. Leadership is always the solution.**
Brian Houston
Spring 2001

Leadership is influence.
John Maxwell

Is there anything worse than a pessimistic spiritual leader?
Lt. Colonel John Hassard

Life

Life is about not knowing, having to change, taking the moment and making the best of it, without knowing what's going to happen next.
Gilda Radner

Simply, simply.
Henry David Thoreau

Hold fast to dreams, for if dreams die life is a broken-winged bird that cannot fly.
Langston Hughes

The great use of life is to spend it for something that will outlast itself.
William James

I can sum life in three words—it goes on.
Robert Frost

May you LIVE all the days of your life.
Jonathan Swift

It's those small daily happenings that make life so spectacular.
Andy Rooney

What I'm concerned about is the people who don't dwell on the meaninglessness of life, or the meaningfulness of it— who just pursue mindless entertainment.
Michael K. Hooker

The idea is to die young as late as possible.
Ashley Montagu

Life isn't fair, but it's still good.
Regina Brett

We seek in the lives of those who went before us the meaning of our lives.
Ardis Whitman

Though no one can go back and make a brand new start, anyone can start from now and make a brand new ending.
Carl Bard

Life is change. Growth is optional. Choose wisely.
Karen Kaiser Clark

Make sure the thing you're living for is worth dying for.
Charles Mayes

Don't look back if you can't smile and don't look forward if you can't dream.
Source Unknown

One of our stated goals for this decade in our lives is to have more time for less things.
Colonel Henry Gareipy

The most important thing in life is knowing God and His place in our lives.
General Eva Burrows (Ret.)
July 28, 2007

Life should not be a promenade of pleasure, but rather it should be a pilgrimage of promise.
Lt. Colonel Paul Bollwahn
June 21, 2006

Birthdays are good for you— the more you have the longer you live.
Greeting Card Sentiment

I read that every happiness of today is a beautiful memory for tomorrow, but I had to watch out that there weren't some tears along the way.

Commissioner Carol Bassett
April 21, 2006

God doesn't call us to observe life. He calls us to participate fully in it.

Major Randall Davis
June 20, 2009

Life isn't about waiting for the storm to pass. It's about learning to dance in the rain.

Scrapbooking quote

The love of Christ can open your eyes and completely change your thinking about what really matters most in life.

Source Unknown

Life Lessons

Life can only be understood by looking backward, but it must be lived by looking forward.
Soren Kierkegaard

No one can hurt your self-esteem without your permission.
Eleanor Roosevelt

We judge ourselves by what we feel capable of doing, while others judge us by what we have already done.
William Wadsworth Longfellow

Never let yesterday use up too much of today.
Will Rogers

Every exit is an entry to someplace else.
Tom Stoppard

Enjoy the little things in life, for one day you'll look back and realize they were the big things.
Antonio Smith

Although you can lead a horse to water but can't make him drink—if you take him there often enough, he'll know where to go when he's thirsty.
Paul Miller
October 16, 2008

I could open a rosebud, Lord, but I would spoil the flower. I can move the hands of the clock but I can't change the time.
Virginia Talmadge

Life is what happens to you while you are making other plans.
Robert Balzer

The difference between a rut and a grave is the depth.
George Duplain

However good or bad a situation is, it will change.
Regina Brett
November 23, 2008

Never judge a book by its movie.
J. W. Eagan

All of our hopes and our dreams for a better tomorrow can be found in the blessings that God has provided for us today.
Charlie DeLeo

The way we teach our children about the value of money is to keep asking them to lend us some.
Major Mark Herbert
March 23, 2003

If you're not doing something with your life, it doesn't matter how long it is.
Peace Corps Commercial

All the flowers of all the tomorrows are in the seeds of today.
Indian proverb

Better bend than break.
Scottish Proverb

Doing the same thing over and over again and expecting a different result is the definition of insanity.
An Alcoholics Anonymous Maxim

It's risky to go out on a limb, but that's where the fruit is.
Our Daily Bread, Dec-Feb, 2002-03

Age doesn't always bring wisdom. Sometimes age comes alone.
Source Unknown

LOVE

Every time you smile at someone, it is an action of love, a gift to that person, a beautiful thing.
Mother Teresa

The greatest happiness of life is the conviction that we are loved, loved for ourselves, or rather in spite of ourselves.
Victor Hugo

Love is an act of endless forgiveness.
Peter Ustinov

It is not how much we do, but how much love we put in the doing. It is not how much we give, but how much love we put in the giving.
Mother Teresa

Love does not consist in gazing at each other, but in looking outward together in the same direction.
Antoine de Saint Exupéry

Love is not only something you feel. It's something you do.
David Wilkerson

It's easy to love the lovable—it's the unlovable we should reach out to.
Joan Kroc

If you judge people, you have no time to love them.
Mother Teresa

So often when we say "I love you" we say it with a huge "I" and a small "you."
Antony

It's a Scriptural truth that without love we are just making a bunch of noise—and it's not the joyful kind. It's the earplug kind.
Major Keith J. Welch

When we sow love we reap a harvest of love and forgiveness from others.
Major Connie Morris
January 11, 2009

The father of the prodigal son wasn't filled with "I told you so." He was filled with compassion.
Major Cheryl Miller
November 1, 2006

It is always the right time to realize that God loves you.
Lt. Colonel Larry Bosh
December 17, 2005

We're commanded to narrate love into being by putting ourselves outside of ourselves and seeing the other person first.
Major Beverly Woodland
July 10, 2003

**I have learned and continue to learn that genuine Christian love is the anchor in my life.
It is God who has made my way perfect.**
Commissioner Rob Saunders (Ret.)
December 19, 2002

Discipline is loving your children now so that other people will love them later.
Major Florence Forster
September 25, 1993

Love in action doesn't create miracles, but it does facilitate them.
Captain Timothy Duperree
May 11, 2008

> *"If you go the wrong way—to the right or to the left—you will hear a voice behind you saying, 'This is the right way. You should go this way.'"*

Isaiah 30:21 (NC)

*W*hen it comes to retracing a new route, some of us are directionally challenged. In the days before MapQuest and GPS, many drivers (notoriously male), would doggedly insist they knew the way, only to end up three expressways and umpteen miles past the right exit. Today, equipped with a GPS system, travelers can hit the road with expert guidance and instant navigational advice. Those who have travelled spiritual routes before us have also left behind key navigational points to follow on the journey to righteous living.

MIND

Whether you think you can or whether you think you can't, you're right.
Henry Ford

If a cluttered desk is the sign of a cluttered mind—of what then is an empty desk?
Albert Einstein

Curiosity is one of the permanent and certain characteristics of a vigorous intellect.
Samuel Johnson

Suffering loosens the rigidity of the mind.
Harold Begbie

A mind, like a home, is furnished by its owner, so if one's life is cold and bare he can blame no one but himself.
Louis L'Amour

We must assess our thoughts and beliefs and reckon whether they are moving us closer to conformity to Christ or farther away from Him.
John Ortberg

No mere intellectual beliefs can save men, because right opinions do not make right hearts.
Catherine Booth

**Some minds are like concrete. Thoroughly mixed up
and permanently set.**
Church sign

Not what you think you are. But what you think, you are.
Source Unknown

MISSION

The worst thing in the world is to have sight and no vision.
Helen Keller

**Use your uniqueness to make a big deal out of God every
day of your life!**
Max Lucado

**Here is a test to see if your mission on earth is finished. If
you're alive—it isn't.**
Francis Bacon

Calcuttas are everywhere, if we only have eyes to see. Find your Calcutta.
Mother Teresa

Jesus never says to the poor, "Come find the church," but He says to those of us in the church, "Go into the world and find the poor, hungry, homeless, imprisoned."
Tony Campolo

When we are out of sympathy with the young, then I think our work in this world is over.
Gordon McDonald

The face of the Son of Man was set on a goal and He would not be deterred regardless of the cost.
Reverend Frank Bernardi
July 1, 2007

Mission is the clear, written way an organization exists and what it seeks to accomplish.
John C. Bowling

The frontline of The Salvation Army must always run through the agony of the world.
Arnold Brown

Make your life a mission—not an intermission.
Arnold H. Glasgow

Where there's a need, go and do something!
William Booth

Lord, help us not to be satisfied with vegetable gardens for our own convenience.
Commissioner Christine MacMillan

Ministry and mission are found in Jesus.
Major George Polarek
April 8, 2009

If a project is good and it is going to make a difference— there will always be opposition.
Lt. Colonel Steve Hedgren
September 17, 2008

My plan as a college student was to work at a wealthy camp where I could teach soccer—but at the Salvation Army's Camp Wonderland I tasted ministry for the first time, and I realized I wanted more.
Major Richard Munn
April 26, 2006

**My mission is to meet needs, heal hurts
and help change lives.**
Major George Polarek
July 30, 2008

**We need to get more fanatical about our
mission around the world.**
Lt. Colonel Roland Sewell
June 5, 2003

**You and I are called to be "missioners" for good — who
hear from God and then go and tell what we
have heard from Him.**
Commissioner Israel Gaither
November 2, 2002

**Christianity is sometimes watered down. Some can sit
in a mega–church and be entertained, but I thank God
for The Salvation Army's mission because God is
using us to help transform lives.**
Commissioner Gisèle Gowans
November 2, 2002

Salvation Army officers are called to comfort the disturbed and disturb the comfortable.
Lt. Colonel Art Smith
September 1988

The Church is being pushed to the margins in this modern age—can we live there? We are called to make a radical difference in the age in which we live! Mission matters most.
Commissioner Israel L. Gaither
August 3, 2003

We must always remember that our ministry to others is "for their sake"—but it is done in Jesus' name.
Major Inger Nygaard
March 19, 2002

Meeting people at the intersection between Scripture and the daily circumstances of life is what differentiates an effective preaching ministry from wasting people's time.
Source Unknown

Music

Music expresses that which cannot be put into words and that which cannot remain silent.
Victor Hugo

A painter paints his pictures on canvas. But musicians paint their pictures on silence.
Leopold Stowski

Church is my favorite place to sing. For me, that's where music matters the most and is the most meaningful.
Jennifer Hudson
Oscar winning actress

I think music in itself is healing. It's an explosive expression of humanity. It's something we are all touched by. No matter what culture we're from, everyone loves music.
Billy Joel

> "So be very careful to act exactly as God commands you. Don't veer off to the right or the left. Walk straight down the road God commands so that you'll have a good life."
>
> Deuteronomy 5:32-33a (NIV)

*B*efore we can leave on our trip we must make adequate preparations at home. We should notify neighbors so they can watch the house and give them contact information so we can be reached in an emergency. The mail needs to be stopped and arrangements made to water the plants or care for a pet. These are details that need attention so that we can have worry free travel. If the past is indeed prelude, the following perspectives may help us prepare for what's ahead.

OBEDIENCE

Prepare us to be willing, Lord.
Commissioner Marilyn Francis
July 31, 2005

While dreams are nice and they get us up in the morning, obedience to God is far more important than marching toward some distant dream that may or may not be part of His plan for us.
Angela Hunt

I've found that the secret to life is to always say "yes" to the Lord.
Cadet David G. Martinez
May 2, 2008

When you say "yes" to God, that is where great joy comes from.
Captain Geffory Crowell
March 8, 2009

The essential thing in life is "long obedience in the same direction."
Lt. Colonel David Jones
September 8, 2002

Obedience starts with the first step.
Source Unknown

OPPORTUNITY

A pessimist is one who makes difficulties of opportunities, and an optimist is one who makes opportunities of his difficulties.
Harry S. Truman

When one door closes another door opens; but we often look so long and so regretfully upon the closed door, that we do not see the ones which open for us.
Alexander Graham Bell

Opportunity is often missed because we are broadcasting when we should be tuning in.
National Safety News
January 29, 2006

> *"Show me the right path,*
> *O Lord; point out the*
> *road for me to follow."*
>
> **Psalm 25:4 (NL)**

*W*hen parents turn over the car keys to
their newly licensed teen, they no doubt
wish they could equip the vehicle with big rubber bumpers. But
parents must accept that their child, who seemed only yesterday
to be driving bumper cars, is ready for the freedom and responsibility of driving. Driving a multi–ton vehicle that can reach incredible speeds in seconds requires first, last, and always an eye to
safety. Knowing right from wrong, choosing good over evil, pursuing love instead of hatred, is the difference between redemption and self-destruction.

PATIENCE

Patience is the companion of wisdom.
St. Augustine

The most useful virtue is patience.
John Dewey

Patience is a most necessary qualification for a business;
many a man would rather you heard his story than
granted his request.
Lord Chesterfield

The most useful virtue is patience.
John Dewey

Patience overcomes everything. The world is his
who has patience.
Proverb

God gave everyone patience. Wise people use it.
Source Unknown

PEACE

True peace is found by a man in the depth of his own heart,
the dwelling place of God.
Johann Tauler

**For peace of mind, resign as general manager
of the universe.**
Larry Eisenberg

**If there is to be any peace, it will come through
being, not having.**
Henry Miller

**Peace is not the absence of conflict, but the ability
to cope with it.**
Source Unknown

PRAYER

**Every new victory that a soul gains is the effect
of a new prayer.**
John Wesley

The fewer words—the better prayer.
Martin Luther

There are many times in a man's life when, regardless of the attitude of the body, the soul is on its knees in prayer.
Victor Hugo

I never seal a letter without putting a prayer under the seal.
Stonewall Jackson

When I stay on my knees, that's when I have power.
George W. Bush

What we see as unanswered prayer wilts our willingness to pray, but we should listen carefully, ask boldly and trust completely.
John Jones
July 8, 2008

If being a Christian is all about having a relationship with God, then prayer isn't merely a means to an end; it is an end in itself.
Glenn Welch

God allows us to pray, then He gives us the gift of expectation to receive what He has to give us.
John Jones
July 8, 2008

The lazy man does not, will not, cannot pray, for prayer demands energy.
E. M. Bounds

Prayers unsaid will always be prayers unanswered.
Charlie DeLeo

God has hard-wired the universe in such a way that He works primarily through prayer.
David Jeremiah
The Prayer Matrix

God has not always answered my prayers. If He had, I would have married the wrong man—several times.
Ruth Bell Graham

Sometimes we're so intent on praying that it becomes all talking and no listening.
John Jones
July 8, 2008

Silence and solitude are not ends in themselves, but can become key ingredients in the development of an intimate, contemplative prayer relationship with Christ.
Aaron White

God is often trying to communicate with us—but how often are we tuned in? It shouldn't just be us talking to God, but we should also be listening to Him. We need to have the line open in a two–way direction.

Major David Whittles
May 2, 2002

Prayer is one of our greatest weapons for change.

Captain Robert Webb
November 12, 2006

If you want to be a gracious person, start by praying. If you want to know what to pray about—look around you.

Major Lilia Alkintor
October 22, 2006

Meditation is slowing down enough to hear God.

Major Bill Madison
January 11, 2009

We live in a time when more prayers are sent up for parking spaces than for the lost people in our own families.

Major John Wilkins
September 2004

The way to appreciate God's secrets is to share yours with Him.
Major Don Osman
May 7, 2003

When we clasp our hands in prayer, it is the beginning of an uprising against the disorder of this world.
Lt. Colonel Lyell Rader
August 21, 2003

Why did Jesus, the Son of God, who needed to pray so little, pray so much—and why do we who need to pray so much, pray so little?
Major James Allison
January 25, 2006

We should commit ourselves to being that one PRAY–er for particular people so that they won't have to wonder if there is someone praying personally for them.
Major Betty Israel
January 10, 2002

Prayer uses all the attitude of human spirit. It is the highest activity of which the human spirit is possible.
Commissioner William Mabena
August 2001

There are times when we feel the need to do things with friends, but there are also times when we need to just sit and listen.
Major Margaret Ousey
March 21, 2001

When we ask God to do something *for* us, He generally wants to do something *in* us.
Source Unknown

> "You have made known to me the path of life; you will fill me with joy in your presence, with eternal pleasures at your right hand."
>
> **Psalm 16:11 (NIV)**

*I*t's essential to step away from our work, stretch our legs, and remember that God is in our very breath. We need to rejuvenate our bodies, minds, and spirits by resting and relaxing, sharing a simple meal with families and friends, and appreciating our blessings. A slower pace instills a reverence for life, for God, our world, and human relationships. In silence and solitude, we can recognize the difference between our needs and wants. This discipline creates the space to identify what separates us from God, and helps us move toward a more intimate relationship with Him.

RELATIONSHIPS

Nothing gives one person so much advantage over another as to remain always cool and unruffled under all circumstances.
Thomas Jefferson

Among those whom I like or admire, I can find no common denominator, but among those whom I love, I can: all of them make me laugh.
W. H. Auden

You can't hold a man down without staying down with him.
Booker T. Washington

Be not angry that you cannot make others as you wish them to be, since you cannot make yourself as you wish to be.
Thomas à Kempis

You must live with people to know their problems and live with God in order to solve them.
P. T. Forsyth

Laughter is the shortest distance between two people.
Victor Borge

No one is useless in this world who lightens the burden of anyone else.
Charles Dickens

A smile is kind of like a tranquilizer without the cost.
Major Betty Israel

Shared laughter creates a bond of friendship. When people laugh together, they cease to be young and old, master and pupils, worker and driver. They have become a single group of human beings, enjoying their existence.
E. Grant Lee

We who fear the Lord need to talk to each other.
Thebisa Chaava
July 23, 2008

When you get into a disagreement with someone—just build a bridge and get over it.
Fred Morsberger

God is either first, or He is nowhere with us individually. The very essence of religion is "God first" and allegiance and obedience to Him first.
Catherine Booth

The keys to our relationships are affirmation and optimism.
Major Gary Miller
September 5, 2007

The question is not who's my neighbor, but whose neighbor am I?
Commissioner Lalkiamlova
April 4, 2008

Our definition of community is that it is a group of diverse people brought together by a common element bearing acceptance and trust.
Captains Leslie Flanders and Jessica DeMichael
September 24, 2007

A relationship with God can only happen when we forego the weak, incorrect messages the world has to offer us.
Captain Mike Harris
July 2, 2006

The nations of the world begin next door these days.
Commissioner Joy Baillee
June 10, 2006

We can't say "Our Father" without acknowledging that we are brothers and sisters.
Commissioner Robert Watson

There is nothing more harmful to the Body of Christ than when Christians are not in harmony with each other.

Commissioner Margaret Sutherland
March 25, 2004

Unity in diversity doesn't happen when diversity is merely tolerated—it comes when diversity is celebrated.

Commissioner Alex Hughes

To abound in hope, we must be an inclusive—not an exclusive Army. As Christ is an inclusive Savior—so we must be an inclusive Army.

Commissioner Margaret Taylor
March 2, 2004

There are three forms of relationship. We move away from people, against people or towards people.

General Eva Burrows (Ret.)
August 11, 2002

Mind the gap ... It is so easy to create a gap between ourselves and God ... There can also sometimes be a gap between ourselves and the people we are called to serve.

Commissioner Gisèle Gowans
May 16, 2002

These days it is possessions that are loved and people that are used.
Major Sharon Baker
April 21, 2002

I actively seek a relationship with Jesus every day.
Major Debbie Sjögren
July 20, 2008

Fellowship means sharing anything together that we have in common concerning the things of Christ.
Major Todd Hawks
February 20, 2008

RESURRECTION

Our Lord has written the promise of the resurrection, not in books alone, but in every leaf in springtime.
Martin Luther

In the presence of the resurrection of Jesus all other miracles pale as do the stars before the rising sun. It is the crowning evidence that He is the Son of God.
Samuel Logan Brengle

The cross is central. It is struck into the middle of the world, into the middle of time, into the middle of destiny. The cross is struck in to the heart of God.
Frederick W. Norwood

The cross is God's centerpiece on the table of time.
Paul C. Guttke

The cross was the greatest rescue operation ever undertaken on behalf of mankind.
Brigadier W. I. C. Dobbie
November 6, 2003

The only thing that can make a new creation is the power of the cross.
Major Earl Fitzgerald
March 19, 2008

> "But those who hope in the Lord will renew their strength. They will soar on wings like eagles; they will run and not grow weary, they will walk and not be faint."
>
> Isaiah 40:31 (NIV)

*T*ravel can be an ordeal for families who fail to plan ahead. On one extended road trip a husband told his wife they would just "find" someplace along the way to spend the night. But there was only one little motel along the highway with vacancies. As the wife pulled back the sheets on the bed, she saw hair and grit, causing her to wonder when the sheets were last changed. She was not happy with her spouse and they had anything but a restful night's sleep! So be sure to make reservations in advance. Perhaps these thoughts will help us avoid surprises along the way that leave us in less than ideal circumstances.

SALVATION

Here is the greatest truth of all: God saves man.
Evangeline Booth

When you look at our world that is so wracked with pain and need, know that all of that takes second place to the world's greatest need—to know Jesus.

Andy Garcia
August 6, 2006

When our depravity meets His divinity,
it's a beautiful collision.

David Crowder

He is no fool who gives away what he cannot keep, to gain what he cannot lose.

Missionary Jim Elliot

Salvation is freedom from darkness. It means liberation from something.

Major Norman Garcia
August 10, 2008

Service

Anyone can be great because anyone can be a servant.
Martin Luther King, Jr.

If you can do more—you should.
Robert Redford
November 4, 2006

Never tell a young person that something cannot be done.
God may have been waiting for countless centuries
for somebody ignorant enough of the impossibility to
do that thing.
John Andrew Holmes

God has no plan B. You're it.
J. B. Hill

Give a man a dollar and you cheer his heart. Give him a
dream and you challenge his heart. Give him Christ and you
change his heart. Then the dollar and the dream become
meaningful to him, and to others.
C. Neil Strait

Find out where God is working and join Him there.
Henry Blackaby

The best exercise for strengthening the heart is reaching down and lifting people up.
Ernest Blevins

End your prayer with—"And is it me, Lord?" We are all called and we are all sent for full time service.
General Shaw Clifton

We are saved to serve, not saved to sit.
Captain Michael Cripe
February 22, 2008

In my calling, my goal must always be to be pure and to be fruitful.
Lt. Colonel Gladys DeMichael
July 11, 2007

We come to serve the servants of the servant Christ.
Lt. Colonel David Jeffrey
July 17, 2007

**Overarching all we do in social services is the
love of Jesus Christ.**
Major Richard Vander Weele
June 27, 2007

**If you think something small cannot make a difference, try
going to sleep with a mosquito in the room.**
African saying
Shared by Lt. Colonel Jolene Hodder

Stop doing the Army and start being the Army.
Commissioner Max Feener
July 19, 2006

**Once Daniel resolved to serve God—it affected all the
decisions he made from then on because biblical values
and beliefs are always going to be challenged in
a pagan culture.**
Major Todd Hawks
April 5, 2006

**We each in our own uniqueness have been taken by God to
play an individual role according to His will.**
Lt. Colonel Mary Petroff
March 8, 2006

When we serve God we serve man, and when we serve man we serve God.
Lt. Colonel Alida Bosshardt
April 6, 2004

There is no room in this world for unemployed Christians.
Major Chet Emmons

We should serve others with grace and tender incentives.
Captain Hollie Leonardi
August 28, 2003

There is no such thing as a secret trumpet player.
Major Mark Herbert
June 22, 2003

As a former firefighter and paramedic—I didn't focus on the dead and the damage at emergency sites, but on the living ... I see Christ in the sacrificial service of our workers at disaster scenes.
Major Mike Olsen
September 12, 2002

God, in His graciousness, tells us to come alongside and work with Him. It is important for us to remember, as I have read, that God plus one is always a majority.
Major Margaret Castley
November 5, 2002

Think of yourself like an ox—between the priest and the altar—ready for service or for sacrifice.
Lt. Colonel Roland Sewell
January 28, 2004

The task of every Christian is to find out what God is doing and ask, "Can I help?"
Source Unknown

SIN

Sin is not hurtful because it is forbidden, but it is forbidden because it is hurtful.
Benjamin Franklin

The worst sin toward our fellow creatures is not to hate them, but to be indifferent to them; that's the essence of inhumanity.
George Bernard Shaw

It was not the apple on the tree that caused the sin—it was the pair on the ground.
Sandy Shaw

Sin is sweet in the beginning, but bitter in the end.
The Talmud

At Adam's fall sin entered the bloodstream of humanity.
Major George Hood
April 9, 2009

Selfishness is the root and cause of all sin.
Major Ed Forster
July 1, 2009

The more sinful a man becomes the more unhappy he becomes.
Major Bill Madison
January 11, 2009

While sin grieves the heart of God and fills His heart with pain … the sin of believers breaks the heart of God.

Commissioner Ronald Irwin

August 1, 2003

SPIRITUAL GROWTH

Heaven never helps the man who will not act.

Sophocles

Satan pushes and condemns. God draws and encourages, and with time and experience we learn the difference.

Richard Foster

The fruit of silence is prayer, the fruit of prayer is faith, the fruit of faith is love, the fruit of love is service, and the fruit of service is peace.

Mother Teresa

A little thing is a little thing, but faithfulness in a little thing becomes a great thing.
Plato

Let each become all that he was created capable of being.
Thomas Carlyle

Consciousness is a gift to be cherished. How wondrous that we grow by becoming conscious of the world and our place in it.
Isaac Bashevis Singer

Personal change begins for each of us when we cry out to God for what God wants for us with open hands and expectant hearts.
Bruce Wilkerson

The ruins of my soul repair—and make my heart a place of prayer.
Charles Wesley

The life that is rightly related to God is as natural as breathing.
Oswald Chambers

Our God desires not only our love and allegiance, but also growth in wisdom, holiness and character.
Jack Madahgian

The exchanged life is—less of me, and more of Him.
Hudson Taylor

Living in Christ involves the total person and demands a conscious, sensitive, moment by moment response to the Spirit of God.
Clarence D. Wiseman

We can't lean on our history with God—we must have daily devotions with Him.
Captain Kenneth Argot
July 20, 2008

I am living each day—trying to give God who I am.
Lt. Colonel Trevor Davis

Are you the person today that you thought you would be when you first believed in Jesus?
Major Bud Ferreira
October 7, 2007

Our free will can be so embraced and changed by the touch of the Spirit that the waywardness of our rebellious nature is brought into conformity with the nature and will of God.
Major Barry Corbitt
June 2006

I find myself learning to dance with Jesus without stepping on his toes.
Major Carole Bate
January 29, 2006

Don't let the scarecrow of "not good enough" keep you from being all that God wants you to be.
Captain Sandra Fisher
March 16, 2003

If plants aren't nurtured—they don't grow and develop. Spiritual power is found in God's strength, security and the fruit we bear. We best live out our spiritual lives by showing the strength of Christ within us.
Captain Stephen Dutfield
October 21, 2001

SPORTS

In life, as in a football game, the principle to follow is:
Hit the line hard.
Theodore Roosevelt

You can learn more character on the two-yard line than
anywhere else in life.
Paul Dietzel, Louisiana State University

When something unexplainable happens (like that catch in
the Super Bowl) I attribute it to God.
David Tyree
New York Giants
February 3, 2008

Failure is part of success.
Hank Aaron

Fear causes people to draw back from situations; it brings
on mediocrity; it dulls creativity; it sets one up to be a
loser in life.
Fran Tarkenton

STRENGTH

Physical strength can never permanently withstand the impact of spiritual force.
Franklin D. Roosevelt

Lord, if you don't come through for us—we come undone.
MacDonald Chaava
August 20, 2006

Now to be more than conqueror is not merely to put down the enemy, but to rise to higher heights upon his prostrate form. To be more than conqueror is not only to withstand the blows of the weapons in the enemy's hands, but also to seize these same weapons and use them in an aggressive attack upon the enemy.
Milton S. Agnew

Life is living, Lord, and living is coping; and coping is knowing how to use one's resources.
Virginia Talmadge

Power and strength ultimately lie within the giving of love.
Major George Hood
March 19, 2008

SUBMISSION

**Most people must struggle and like Jacob struggle with the
angel until the morning dawns, the active way wherein the
will must be subjected bit by bit, piecemeal
and progressively, to the divine will.**
Thomas Kelly

**There are two kinds of people: Those who say to God,
"Thy will be done," and those to whom God says, "All
right then, have it your way."**
C. S. Lewis

**Submit to the hand of the divine Potter, become as clay in
His hands, and out of the ugliness and distortion of the
past He will make for Himself a vessel of honor.**
Robert Hoggard

**The greatness of a man's power is in the
measure of his surrender.**
William Booth

A life of total surrender equals a life of complete victory.
Major James Allison
October 8, 2006

**The human part of me would always choose comfort over
sacrifice every time. But I claim freedom to commit
myself to Christ.**
Major Chrissy Rock
May 10, 2006

**Dear God, Your will—nothing more,
nothing less, nothing else.**
*—a prayer by Bobby Richardson
quoted by Major Tim Lyle*
March 5, 2006

**The greatest obstacle in our knowing and experiencing the
love of God, the forgiveness and pardon of our sins,
is our stubborn will.**
Major Don Osman
August 28, 1994

When you put your little nothing in God's hands—He multiplies it. Stop talking about your inadequacies and give God what you've got!
General John Gowans (Ret.)
November 2, 2002

In being nothing, we become something.
Captain Adrian Allman
May 23, 2002

I believe my willingness to say "yes" was the key that opened the doors to the way that God has used me.
Commissioner Carol Saunders
September 19, 2002

SUCCESS

I have learned that success is to be measured not so much by the position that one has reached in life as by the obstacles which he has overcome while trying to succeed.
Booker T. Washington

To accomplish great things, we must not only act but also dream, and not only plan but also believe.
Anatole France

The road to success is always under construction.
Lily Tomlin

Success consists of getting up just one more time than you fall.
Oliver Goldsmith

Success is a journey, not a destination. The doing is often more important than the outcome.
Arthur Ashe

Start by doing what's necessary, then what's possible, and suddenly you are doing the impossible.
Francis of Assisi

Believe you can and you're halfway there.
Theodore Roosevelt

Great things are not done by impulse, but by a series of small things brought together.
Vincent Van Gogh

**If we all did the things we are capable of,
we would astound ourselves.**
Thomas Edison

**Success is when I add value to myself. Significance is when
I add value to others.**
John Maxwell

**The secret of success is a heart consumed with the flame
of ardent, holy, heavenly love.**
William Booth

A Christian formula for victory is God can if I will.
Major Don Osman

There is no elevator to success; you have to take the stairs.
Source Unknown

SUFFERING

**God whispers to us in our pleasures, but shouts
to us in our pain.**
C.S. Lewis

I am richer since I lived with pain. My list'ning ear grown sensitive receives deeper and higher and far sweeter tones than those I used to hear.
Catherine Baird

If I can understand how He suffered for me, I can better understand what He does for me.
Corps Sergeant Major CeCe Coffer
April 7, 2009

Jesus understands suffering.
Lt. Colonel Dan Starrett
April 7, 2009

I pursued pleasure hoping it would ease the pain, but it didn't, only Christ could ease my pain.
Accepted Candidate John Luby
August 3, 2007

There is a grief that can't be spoken.
Les Miserables

> *"Even when the way goes through Death Valley, I'm not afraid when you walk at my side."*
>
> Psalm 23:4a (MSG)

No matter how carefully we plan our route, we are bound at some point to wind up off course. That sudden detour, the cul-de-sac we thought was an on–ramp, the white out conditions, loom unexpectedly and force us to recalculate our destination. It's like that in our spiritual life, too. And it can seem so unfair. Yet God uses all experiences, whether they be road closings or traffic jams, to help us re-evaluate and correct our priorities and our path.

TEMPTATION

Satan tries to come at us from every possible direction—
just as he did when he tried to tempt Jesus.

Captain Joe Burton
March 15, 2006

Man's law often allows what God's law prohibits.
Major G. Howard Palomaki

Opportunity may knock once, but temptation bangs on your door continually.
Church Sign

TIME

Do not squander time for that is the stuff life is made of.
Benjamin Franklin

We need time to dream, time to remember and time to reach the infinite.
Gladys Taber

We live in the era between the already and the not yet.
Commissioner Margaret Sutherland
October 3, 2002

TRUST

I have learned that faith means trusting in advance what will only make sense in reverse.
Philip Yancey

It is always wise to look ahead, but difficult to look beyond what we can see.
Winston Churchill

I have history with God, and I trust Him in all things.
Karen Downing
November 4, 2007

Trust is born out of relationship. It is forged by experience.
Phil Barrett
June 21, 2009

Faith is not needing to know everything God knows, but trusting that God knows everything.
Dorothy Albelo

For your heart, as for mine, the question is not do I understand God, but do I trust Him?
Catherine Bramwell Booth

David didn't know how he was going to get on with Goliath—but trusting God for the results he moved on to face his reality.
Lt. Colonel Sylvia Dalziel
September 12, 2002

It is the time when we question, "Does God reign?" that we need to place our dependence on Him.
Major Joan Canning
January 21, 2009

God promises to watch over us and make the path clear for us. All we have to do is trust.
Major Nancy Banfield
February 21, 2007

The one who experiences renewal is the one who is willing to place her utter dependence on God.
Major Joan Canning
January 21, 2009

We are wasting our time if we are regretting the past or worrying about the future. Trust God for the present.
Captain Carolyn Webb
November 4, 2007

TRUTH

The content of a word that is truly from God will always conform to and be consistent with the truths about God's nature and Kingdom that are made clear in the Bible.
Dallas Willard

To be persuasive we must be believable; to be believable we must be credible; to be credible we must be truthful.
Edward R. Murrow

One of the hardest things in this world is to admit you are wrong. And nothing is more helpful in resolving a situation than its frank admission.
Benjamin Disraeli

The angels may have wider spheres of action and nobler forms of duty than ourselves, but truth and right to them and to us are the same thing.
E. H. Chapin

A man can never hope to be more than he is if he is not first honest about what he isn't.
Don Williams

No man can produce great things who is not thoroughly sincere in dealing with himself.
James Russell Lowell

If you're going to be sincere—be sincere and right.
Alice Shaw Clifton

The truth is Jesus Christ.
Captain Michael Harris
September 2, 2007

Jesus loves me enough to tell me the truth.
Lt. Colonel Judy Falin
June 20, 2007

It takes a lot of words to float a lie, but the truth just is.
Lieutenant Tarryl Ray
April 13, 1997

You cannot change the truth, but the truth can change you.
Source Unknown

> *"You're blessed when you stay on course [traveling] steadily on the road revealed by God."*
>
> Psalm 119:1 (MSG)

Sometimes we will venture into uncharted waters, but if we are securely anchored in our faith, we'll survive even a category 5 hurricane. Just when we become accustomed to a life without signs and wonders, unexpected discoveries will surprise us— genuine repentance, a new point of view, a relationship that seems finally to have clicked. We'll see grace at every turn in the road. Learning from our mistakes will prevent us from retracing old paths that lead only to misery and pain. We'll stop retreating to the past, celebrate each day and keep moving forward.

WHOLENESS

Always be a first-rate version of yourself, instead of a second-rate version of somebody else.
Judy Garland

God can do wonders with a broken heart if you give
Him all the pieces.
Victor Alfsen

God can take anything that's broken and make it whole. But
you must give Him the pieces, because He's the Creator.
And He can take all the pieces and make them fit together.
From the television program Touched By An Angel

When we are shattered we find that the pieces will never
exactly fit back together again. Spaces are left where God
and others can find a way to enter in.
Source Unknown

WISDOM

The better informed, the wiser and more cultivated we are,
provided we're dedicated wholly to God, the more
effectually we can glorify God and serve our fellowmen.
Samuel Logan Brengle

None of us is as smart as all of us.
Lt. Colonel Donald Faulkner
April 7, 2008

One of the true evidences of real wisdom is the ability to see our mistakes.
Catherine Bramwell Booth

Look for and find wisdom. For wisdom is of God, and not of man.
Major Dorothy Hitzka
January 17, 2007

Wisdom is the right use of knowledge.
From Chosen To Be A Soldier

A wise man knows everything; a shrewd one, everybody.
Source Unknown

WITNESS

Living the Gospel is always more meaningful than merely talking about it.
Frederick Coutts

It doesn't hurt to be a testimony.
Marion Erickson
May 30, 2008

We are called to be candles in the darkness—lights for those who don't know The Way.
Major Mark Tillsley
August 19, 2008

When we testify, we are saying, "Do it again, Lord."
Major Carole Bate
June 9, 2007

We have an unending opportunity to reach out and touch others in the name of Jesus. God intends to touch people through us.
Captain Steve Morris
February 7, 2007

God raised up The Salvation Army to be a voice in the community—very often it is a voice without words.
Commissioner Christine MacMillan
July 30, 2006

You don't have to be a star to shine. For it was the ministry of just a lit candle that a woman used to find her lost piece of silver.
A prisoner

WORK

The task ahead of us is never as great as the Power behind us.
Ralph Waldo Emerson

There is no substitute for hard work.
Thomas Edison

My grandfather once told me that there are two kinds of people: those who do the work and those who take the credit. He told me to try to be in the first group; there was much less competition there.
Indira Ghandi

If you have built castles in the air, your work need not be lost—that is where they should be. Now put foundations under them.
Henry David Thoreau

Between the great things that we cannot do and the small things we will not do, the danger is that we shall do nothing.
Adolph Monod

Far and away the best prize that life offers is the chance to work hard at work worth doing.
Theodore Roosevelt

What is written without effort is in general read without pleasure.
Samuel Johnson

Doing heart work is hard work.
Dr. Linda Burkle

Your true vocation lies where your talents and the needs of the world cross.
Aristotle

There are two ways of getting what we want—by working harder and harder or by simply wanting less.
G. K. Chesterton

I never did a day's work in my life—it was all fun.
Thomas Edison

Labor, if it were not necessary for the existence, would be indispensable for the happiness of man.
Samuel Johnson

We have a saying around our house that to do God's will is to do the next thing.
Gloria Gaither
January 2003

Don't get so busy doing the work of the Lord, that you forget the Lord of the work.
Colonel Tom Lewis
February 6, 2008

Man is happy only as he finds a work worth doing—and does it well.
E. Merrill Root

The Lord has called us to a great work. We must not be content with a small one.
William Booth

Toil brings no shame to those who do it in His holy name.
Lt. Colonel Will Clark

Lord, you do the work—whether it is to challenge, to reprimand or to comfort. Please, Lord, do the work that's right for us.
Major Barbara Lyne
May 18, 2003

If your work is for the Master, people will follow you. If it is for yourself, they will walk away.
Major Richard Amick

WORSHIP

The Greek word for worship can be interpreted to come forward and kiss.
David Watson

Mary, Martha's sister in the Bible, had it right. She sat at the feet of Jesus.
Captain Amy Argot

My visit to the Western Wall (in Jerusalem) made me question the walls in my life that keep me from worshipping God.
Major Robert Gauthier
April 1, 2008

Work without worship is a serious danger in the church. Worship should always lead to sacrificial service.
Lt. Colonel Clive Adams
August 19, 2008

It is in the hearts and homes of God's people that He is given the highest place.
Commissioner Helen Clifton
August 19, 2008

We all need to be wedded to worship, and real worship is taking joyful delight in the Lord.
Major Janice Fitzgerald
September 21, 2006

One of the purposes of worship is to keep us spiritually awake. If we want to be the spiritual fighting force that we were meant to be—we must be vitally, spiritually awake.
Lt. Colonel Peder Refstie
May 6, 2004

Right relationships are a prerequisite to worship.
Commissioner Margaret Sutherland
March 25, 2004

Worship ought to be something that is sacrificial, that honors God and that is done with obedient hearts.
Major Robin McIntosh
March 18, 2004

List of Contributors

Author Last	Author First
Aaron	Hank
Adams	Scott
Adams	Douglas
Adams	Lt. Colonel Clive
Adams	Thomas
Aesop	
Agnew	Milton
Ajubiga	Major Caroline
Albelo	Dorothy
Alfsen	Victor
Alkintor	Major Lilia
Alkintor	Major Yvon
Allemand	Lt. Colonel Gustave
Allison	Major James
Allman	Captain Adrian
Amick	Major Richard
Anderson	Captain Christine
Anderson	Kerri
Angelou	Maya
Antony	
Argot	Captain Amy
Argot	Captain Kenneth
Aristotle	

Author Last	Author First
Ashe	Arthur
Assisi	Francis of
Atkinson	Major David
Auden	W. H.
Aurelius	Marcus
Ayling	Major Peter
Bacon	Francis
Bailey	Joseph
Baillee	Commissioner Joy
Baird	Catherine
Baker	Major Sharon
Balzer	Robert
Bamford	Major William
Banfield	Major Nancy
Barber	Sharon
Barclay	William
Bard	Carl
Barrett	Phil
Barrie	James M.
Barrington	Major Suzanne
Barrington	Major Tony
Barth	Karl
Bartlett	Lt. Colonel Royston
Bassett	Commissioner Carol
Bate	Major Carole
Bedio	Scott

Author Last	Author First
Beecher	Henry Ward
Bell	Alexander Graham
Bell	Major Mark
Bell	Ruth Graham
Bellamy	Carol
Bennett	Bo
Begbie	Harold
Berle	Milton
Bernardi	Reverend Frank
Berry	Lt. Colonel Sharon E.
Blackaby	Henry
Blevins	Ernest
Bogomoletz	Alexander A.
Bohn	H. G.
Boice	James Montgomery
Bok	Derek
Bollwahn	Lt. Colonel Paul
Bonaparte	Napoleon
Bonhoeffer	Dietrich
Bonnell	John Sutherland
Bono	
Boorstin	Daniel
Booth	Catherine
Booth	Catherine Bramwell
Booth	Evangeline
Booth	Florence

Author Last	Author First
Booth	William
Borge	Victor
Bosh	Lt. Colonel Larry
Bosshardt	Lt. Colonel Alida
Bounds	E. M.
Bowles	William Lisle
Bowling	John C.
Bradbury	William B.
Bradstreet	Anne
Brengle	Samuel Logan
Brett	Regina
Brock	Fred
Broome	Major Eugene
Brown	Arnold
Browning	Major Doug
Bukiewicz	Major Ralph
Burgmayer	Katie
Burkle	Dr. Linda
Burr	Major Doug
Burrows (Ret.)	General Eva
Burton	Captain Joe
Bus	Ralph
Bush	George W.
Bushnell	Horace
Butler	Samuel
Cain	Major Paul

Author Last	Author First
Campolo	Tony
Canning	Major Joan
Carlyle	Thomas
Carmen	
Carpenter	George
Carter	Nate
Carter	Jimmy
Castley	Major Margaret
Chaava	Thebisa
Chaava	MacDonald
Chambers	Oswald
Chapin	E. H.
Chesham	Sally
Chesterfield	Lord
Chesterton	G. K.
Churchill	Winston
Clark	Nolan
Clark	Frank A.
Clark	Karen Kaiser
Clark	Lt. Colonel Will
Clement	Major Christine
Clifton	Commissioner Helen
Clifton	General Shaw
Cocteau	Jean
Coffer	Corps Sergeant Major Ce Ce
Collins	Captain Trista

Author Last	Author First
Colson	Charles
Cooper	Colonel Joy
Corbitt	Major Barry
Cosby	Bill
Coutts	Frederick
Cripe	Captain Michael
Crowder	David
Crowell	Captain Geffory
Dalziel	Lt. Colonel Sylvia
Davis	Elmer
Davis	Lt. Colonel Trevor
Davis	Major Randall
Dean	Harry
Defibaugh	Major Sandra
DeLeo	Charlie
DeMichael	Captain Jessica
DeMichael	Lt. Colonel Gladys
DeMichael	Lt. Colonel Joseph
Dent	James
DeVries	Peter
Dewey	John
Dickens	Charles
Dickinson	Emily
Dickson	Major David
Dietzel	Paul
Dillard	Annie

Author Last	Author First
Disraeli	Benjamin
Dobbie	Brigadier W. I. C.
Dobson	Dr. James
Dodge	Sue
Donaldson	Hal
Downing	Karen
Drucker	Peter
du Plessis	Commisioner Paul
Duke	Jerry
Dulles	John Foster
Duperree	Captain Timothy
Duplain	George
Dutfield	Captain Stephen
Eagan	J. W.
Eagle	Iron
Edison	Thomas
Edwards	Commissioner David
Eims	Leroy
Einstein	Albert
Eisenberg	Larry
Eisenhower	Dwight
Elliot	George
Elliot	Missionary Jim
Elliston	George
Emerson	Ralph Waldo
Emmons	Major Chet

Author Last	Author First
Erickson	Marion
Exupery	Antoine de Saint
Falin	Lt. Colonel John
Falin	Lt. Colonel Judy
Faulkner	Lt. Colonel Donald
Feener	Commissioner Max
Ferguson	Marilyn
Ferreira	Major Bud
Fisher	Captain Sandra
Fitzgerald	Major Earl
Fitzgerald	Major Janice
Flanders	Captain Leslie
Ford	Henry
Forster	Major Ed
Forster	Major Florence
Forsyth	P. T.
Foster	Richard
France	Anatole
Francis	Captain Annalise
Francis	Commissioner Marilyn
Franklin	Benjamin
Frey	Bishop
Fripp	Captain Marian
Frost	Robert
Fuller	Thomas
Gaither	Commissioner Israel L.

Author Last	Author First
Gaither	Gloria
Gaither	William
Garcia	Andy
Garcia	Major Norman
Gardner	John W.
Gareipy	Colonel Henry
Garland	Judy
Gaudion	Major Richard
Gauthier	Major Robert
Ghandi	Indira
Gilliard	Alfred J.
Gilliard	Steve
Gilman	Charlotte Perkins
Glasgow	Arnold H.
Goethe	
Goldsmith	Oliver
Good	Gerald
Gosteli-Porret	Major Evelyne
Gowans	Commissioner Gisèle
Gowans (Ret.)	General John
Graham	Anne
Graham	Billy
Gray	Tabitha
Graybeal	Lynda L.
Green	Dr. Roger
Grey	Larry

Author Last	Author First
Gulliksen	Commissioner Thorleif
Guttke	Paul C.
Guyon	Jeanne
Gyertson	Dr. David J.
Halifax	Lord
Hall	Clarence W.
Hallock	Captain Jacqueline
Hammarskjold	Dag
Hardt	Elaine
Harris	Captain Michael
Harris	Everett
Harris	Sydney J.
Harvey	Paul
Hassard	Lt. Colonel John
Haupt	Lt. Colonel Suzanne
Haupt	Major Gary
Hawks	Captain Bethany
Hawks	Major Todd
Hawthorne	Nathaniel
Hedgren	Lt. Colonel Steve
Hemingway	Ernest
Henrick	George R.
Herbert	Major Mark
Higgs	Liz Curtis
Hill	J. B.
Hill	Jonathan

Author Last	Author First
Himes	Captain Mike
Hitzka	Major Dorothy
Hock	Dee
Hodder	Lt. Colonel Jolene
Hodgson	Rudolph
Hoggard	Robert
Holmes	John Andrew
Holmes	Oliver Wendell
Honeyball	Brigadier Clifford
Hood	Major Donna
Hood	Major George
Hooker	Michael K.
Houston	Brian
Howard	Reverend Roy
Hudson	Jennifer
Hughes	Commissioner Alex
Hughes	Langston
Hugo	Victor
Hunt	Angela
Hutchins	Jan
Irwin	Commissioner Ronald
Israel	Major Betty
Israel	Major Carolee
Israel	Major Mark
Israel	Mary
Jackson	Stonewall

Author Last	Author First
Jackson	Mahalia
James	William
Jefferson	Thomas
Jeffrey	Colonel David
Jeremiah	David
Joel	Billy
Johnson	Samuel
Jones	John
Jones	Lt. Colonel David
Jones	Major Doug
Jones	Major Linda
Jones-Gage	Cheryl
Justvig	Major Richard
Kang	Joshua Choomin
Keller	Helen
Kelly	Thomas
Kempis	Thomas à
Kennedy	John F.
Kennedy	Robert F.
Kettering	Charles
Kierkegaard	Soren
Kilcher	Jewell
King Jr.	Martin Luther
Kingsley	Charles
Knous	Cadet Raymond
Kozol	Jonathan

Author Last	Author First
Krasner	Lee
Kroc	Joan
Kuhlman	Katherine
L'Amour	Louise
Laeger	Major David
Lake	John G.
Lalkiamlova	Commissioner
Lamb	Charles
Larson	Doug
Larsson	Flora
Law	William
Lawson	Douglas M.
Lee	E. Grant
Leidzen	Erik
Leonard	Patrick
Leonardi	Captain Hollie
Leslie	Major Victor
Lessin	Roy
Letterman	Elmer G.
Lewis	C. S.
Lewis	Colonel Tom
Liddon	H. P.
Lincoln	Abraham
Litherland	Major Harry
Lofgren	Colonel Edith
Longfellow	William Wadsworth

Author Last	Author First
Lowell	James Russell
Luby	Accepted Candidate John
Lucado	Max
Luther	Martin
Lyle	Major Tim
Lyne	Major Alan
Lyne	Major Barbara
Mabena	Commissioner William
Mabie	Hamilton Wright
MacArthur	John
MacDonald	George
MacMillan	Commisioner Christine
Madahgian	Jack
Madison	Major Bill
Marshall	Catherine
Marshall	Harold James
Martinez	Cadet David G.
Massieu	Jean Baptiste
Matthes	Rick
Maturin	Basil W.
Maugham	Somerset
Maxwell	Commissioner Earl
Maxwell	John
Mayes	Charles
McCombe	Major Beverly
McDonald	Gordon

Author Last	Author First
McIntosh	Major Robin
McMillan	Major Susan
Meldrum	Major Margaret
Meltzer	Bernard
Merton	Thomas
Millard	Reverend Jonathan
Miller	Calvin
Miller	Commissioner Andrew S.
Miller	John Homer
Miller	Major Cheryl
Miller	Major Gary
Miller	Henry
Miller	Paul
Monfort	F. C.
Monod	Adolph
Montague	Ashley
Montesquieu	
Moretz	Commissioner Lawrence R.
Morris	Captain Wendy
Morris	Major Connie
Morris	Major Steve
Morsberger	Fred
Moulton	Geoff
Munn	Major Richard
Murr	Hugh
Murray	Andrew

Author Last	Author First
Murrow	Edward R.
Newsome	Major Algerome
Nightingale	Earl
Norwich	Julian of
Norwood	Frederick W.
Nweke	Lt. Colonel Beatrice
Nygaard	Major Inger
O'Connor	Flannery
Oalang	Captain Elsa
Ogilvy	Lloyd
Oke	Jeanette
Olsen	Major Mike
Ortberg	John
Orsborn	Albert
Osman	Major Don
Ousey	Major Margaret
Paine	Thomas
Pallant	Captain Dean
Palomaki	Major G. Howard
Paterson	Sir Alexander
Paton	Ann
Patton	George S.
Payne	Major Diane
Peterson	Eugene
Petrie	Ferd
Petroff	Lt. Colonel Mary

Author Last	Author First
Phillips	Michael
Pigford	Lt. Colonel Edith
Pigford	Lt. Colonel Eugene
Plato	
Poff	Major Christine
Poke	Lt. Colonel Victor
Polarek	Major George
Powell	Colin
Presley	Corps Sgt.- Major Cotton
Pressland	Colonel Michael
Purkiser	W. T.
Rader	Commissioner Kay
Rader	Lt. Colonel Herb
Rader	Lyell
Rader	Lt. Colonel Lyell
Rader (Ret.)	General Paul
Radner	Gilda
Ravenhill	Leonard
Ray	Lt. Tarryl
Redford	Robert
Reeves	Christopher
Refstie	Lt. Colonel Peder
Reiland	Dr. Dan
Repass	Captain David
Rice	Condoleezza
Richardson	Bobby

Author Last	Author First
Rickenbacker	Eddie
Riley	Pat
Ringle	Major Ed
Robertson	Sharon
Robinson	Jackie
Rock	Major Chrissy
Rockefeller	John D.
Rogers	Will
Roller	Julia L.
Rooney	Andy
Roosevelt	Eleanor
Roosevelt	Franklin D.
Roosevelt	Theodore
Root	E. Merrill
Roy	Reverend Howard
Ryder	Colonel Myrtle
Sanford	Captain Chris
Saunders	Commissioner Carol
Saunders	Commissioner Rob
Schabacker	Ruth Ann
Schurink	Commissioner Reinder
Scroggie	Graham
Senft	Major Joanne
Sewell	Lt. Colonel Dawn
Sewell	Lt. Colonel Roland
Shaw	Alice

Author Last	Author First
Shaw	George Bernard
Shaw	Sandy
Shoemaker	Samuel
Simington	Richard
Singer	Isaac Bashevis
Sjögren	Major Debbie
Sjögren	Major Randall
Smedes	Lewis
Smith	Antonio
Smith	Captain Allister
Smith	Lt. Colonel Art
Smith	Major Peter
Smyth	Major Janys
Sophocles	
St. Augustine	
Stanford	Charles
Starrett	Lt. Colonel Dan
Starrett	Lt. Colonel Helen
Stead	W. T.
Stevenson	Robert Louis
Stoppard	Tom
Stott	John
Stowell	Joseph
Stowski	Leopold
Strait	C. Neil
Suarez	Major Alberto

Author Last	Author First
Sutherland	Commissioner Margaret
Swanson	Commissioner Sue
Swift	Jonathan
Swindoll	Charles
Taber	Gladys
Talmadge	Virginia
Tarkenton	Fran
Tauler	Johann
Taylor	Commissioner Brian
Taylor	Commissioner Margaret
Taylor	Hudson
Taylor	Lt. Colonel Joy
Templeton	Sir John
Teresa	Mother
Thompson	Lisa
Thoreau	Henry David
Thornhill	Major Fred
Thornton	Major Janey
Tillsley	Major Mark
Tillsley (Ret.)	General Bramwell
Tomlin	Lily
Torrey	R. A.
Tozer	A. W.
Tripp	Bramwell
Tripp	Paul
Truman	Harry S.

Author Last	Author First
Tuck	Commissioner Trevor
Tucker	Emma Booth
Tutu	Desmond
Twain	Mark
Tyree	David
Ustinov	Peter
Van Gogh	Vincent
Van Sickle	Bill
Vander Weele	Major Richard
Varghese	Major David
Wahlstrom	Jarl
Waldrip	Mary H.
Ward	William Arthur
Washington	Booker T.
Washington	George
Watson	Commissioner Robert
Watson	David
Webb	Captain Carolyn
Webb	Captain Robert
Webb	Christopher
Welch	Glenn
Welch	Major Keith J.
Welsh	Major Mark
Wesley	Charles
Wesley	John
White	Aaron

Author Last	Author First
White	Lt. Colonel Charles
Whitman	Ardis
Whittles	Major David
Wilkerson	Bruce
Wilkerson	David
Wilkins	Major John
Willard	Dallas
Williams	Don
Williams	Lt. Colonel Mike
Williams	Marianne
Wilson	Earl
Wiseman	Clarence D.
Wood	Major Graham
Woodland	Major Beverly
Wyman	Mark
Yancey	Philip
Yoder	Captain Stephen
Yoshida	Commissioner Makoto
Zellar	Hubert van
Zeller	John

Crest  *Books*

Salvation Army National Publications

Crest Books, a division of The Salvation Army's National Publications department, was established in 1997 so contemporary Salvationist voices could be captured and bound in enduring form for future generations, to serve as witnesses to the continuing mission of the Army.

Shaw Clifton, *Never the Same Again: Encouragement for New and Not–So–New Christians*, 1997

Compilation*, Christmas Through the Years: A War Cry Treasury*, 1997

William Francis, *Celebrate the Feasts of the Lord: The Christian Heritage of the Sacred Jewish Festivals*, 1998

Marlene Chase, *Pictures from the Word*, 1998

Joe Noland, *A Little Greatness*, 1998

Lyell M. Rader, *Romance & Dynamite: Essays on Science & the Nature of Faith*, 1998

Shaw Clifton, *Who Are These Salvationists? An Analysis for the 21st Century*, 1999

Compilation, *Easter Through the Years: A War Cry Treasury*, 1999

Terry Camsey, *Slightly Off Center! Growth Principles to Thaw Frozen Paradigms*, 2000

Philip Needham, *He Who Laughed First: Delighting in a Holy God* (in collaboration with Beacon Hill Press, Kansas City), 2000

Henry Gariepy, ed., *A Salvationist Treasury: 365 Devotional Meditations from the Classics to the Contemporary*, 2000

Marlene Chase, *Our God Comes: And Will Not Be Silent*, 2001

A. Kenneth Wilson, *Fractured Parables: And Other Tales to Lighten the Heart and Quicken the Spirit*, 2001

Carroll Ferguson Hunt, *If Two Shall Agree* (in collaboration with Beacon Hill Press, Kansas City), 2001

John C. Izzard, *Pen of Flame: The Life and Poetry of Catherine Baird*, 2002

Henry Gariepy, *Andy Miller: A Legend and a Legacy*, 2002

Compilation, *A Word in Season: A Collection of Short Stories*, 2002

R. David Rightmire, *Sanctified Sanity: The Life and Teaching of Samuel Logan Brengle*, 2003

Chick Yuill, *Leadership on the Axis of Change*, 2003

Compilation, *Living Portraits Speaking Still: A Collection of Bible Studies*, 2004

A. Kenneth Wilson, *The First Dysfunctional Family: A Modern Guide to the Book of Genesis*, 2004

Allen Satterlee, *Turning Points: How The Salvation Army Found a Different Path*, 2004

David Laeger, *Shadow and Substance: The Tabernacle of the Human Heart*, 2005

Check Yee, *Good Morning China*, 2005

Marlene Chase, *Beside Still Waters: Great Prayers of the Bible for Today*, 2005

Roger J. Green, *The Life & Ministry of William Booth* (in collaboration with Abingdon Press, Nashville), 2006

Norman H. Murdoch, *Soldiers of the Cross: Susie Swift and David Lamb, 2006*

Henry Gariepy, *Israel L. Gaither: Man with a Mission*, 2006

R.G. Moyles (ed.), *I Knew William Booth, 2007*

John Larsson, *Saying Yes to Life*, 2007

Frank Duracher, *Smoky Mountain High*, 2007

R.G. Moyles, *Come Join Our Army*, 2008

Ken Elliott, *The Girl Who Invaded America: The Odyssey of Eliza Shirley*, 2008

Ed Forster, *101 Everyday Sayings from the Bible*, 2008

Harry Williams, *An Army Needs An Ambulance*, 2009

No Longer Missing: Compelling True Stories from The Salvation Army's Missing Persons Ministry, compiled by Judith Brown and Christine Poff

All titles by Crest Books can be purchased through your nearest Salvation Army Supplies and Purchasing department:

ATLANTA, GA — (800) 786–7372
DES PLAINES, IL — (800) 937–8896
LONG BEACH, CA — (800) 937–8896
WEST NYACK, NY — (888) 488–4882